© *Underwood and Underwood, N. Y.*   *British Official Photo.*
JERUSALEM DELIVERED
On December 11, 1917, the Holy City was entered by the British forces. Following the custom of the Crusaders, General Allenby, commander of the British and Allied forces, made his entry, with his staff and Allied officers, through the Jaffa Gate, on foot.

COMPLETE EDITION

HISTORY OF THE WORLD WAR

An Authentic Narrative of
The World's Greatest War

By FRANCIS A. MARCH, Ph.D.
In Collaboration with
RICHARD J. BEAMISH
Special War Correspondent
and Military Analyst

With an Introduction
By GENERAL PEYTON C. MARCH
Chief of Staff of the United States Army

With Exclusive Photographs by
JAMES H. HARE and DONALD THOMPSON
World-Famed War Photographers
and with Reproductions from the Official Photographs of the United States, Canadian, British, French and Italian Governments

MCMXIX
LESLIE-JUDGE COMPANY
New York

Copyright, 1918

FRANCIS A. MARCH

This history is an original work and is fully
protected by the copyright laws, including the
right of translation. All persons are warned
against reproducing the text in whole or in
part without the permission of the publishers.

CONTENTS

VOLUME V

CHAPTER I. REDEMPTION OF THE HOLY LAND

A Long Campaign Progressing Through Hardships to Glory—General Allenby Enters Jerusalem on Foot—Turkish Army Crushed in Palestine—Battle of Armageddon . . 1

CHAPTER II. TRANSPORTATION PROBLEMS

Government Ownership of Railroads, Telegraphs, Telephones—Getting the Men from Training Camps to the Battle Fronts—From Texas to Toul—A Gigantic System Working Without a Hitch 10

CHAPTER III. SHIPS AND THE MEN WHO MADE THEM

The Emergency Fleet Corporation—Charles M. Schwab as Master Shipbuilder—Hog Island the Wonder Shipyard of the World—An Unbeatable Record—Concrete Ships—Wooden Ships—Standardizing the Steel Ship—Attitude of Labor in the War—Samuel Gompers an Unofficial Member of the Cabinet—Great Task of the United States Employment Service 23

CHAPTER IV. GERMANY'S DYING DESPERATE EFFORT

The High Tide of German Success—An Army of Six Million Men Flung Recklessly on the Allies—Most Terrific Battles in all History—The Red Ruin of War from Arras to St. Quentin—Amiens Within Arms' Reach of the Invaders—Paris Bombarded by Long-Range Guns from Distance of Seventy-six Miles—A Generalissimo at Last—Marshal Foch in Supreme Command 43

CONTENTS

CHAPTER V. CHÂTEAU-THIERRY, FIELD OF GLORY PAGE

German Wave Stops with the Americans—Prussian Guard Flung Back—The Beginning of Autocracy's End—America's Record of Valor and Victory—Cantigny—Belleau Wood—Thierry—St. Mihiel—Shock Troops of the Enemy Annihilated—Soldier's Remarkable Letter 73

CHAPTER VI. ENGLAND AND FRANCE STRIKE IN THE NORTH

Second Terrific Blow of General Foch—Lens, the Storehouse of Minerals Captured—Bapaume Retaken—British Snap the Famous Hindenburg Line—The Great Thrust Through Cambrai—Tanks to the Front—Cavalry in Action . . 103

CHAPTER VII. BELGIUM'S GALLANT EFFORT

The Little Army Under King Albert Thrusts Savagely at the Germans—Ostend and Zeebrugge Freed from the Submarine Pirates—Pathetic Scenes as Belgians are Restored to their Homes 120

CHAPTER VIII. ITALY'S TERRIFIC DRIVE

Enemy Offensive Opens on Front of Ninety-seven Miles—Repulse of the Austrians—Italy Turns the Tables—Terrific Counter-Thrusts from the Piave to Trente—Forcing the Alpine Passages—Battles High in the Air—English, French and Americans Back up the Italians in Humbling the Might of Austria—D'Annunzio's Romantic Bombardment of Vienna—Diaz Leads His Men to Victory 139

CHAPTER IX. BULGARIA DESERTS GERMANY

Greece in the Throes of Revolution—Fall of Constantine—Serbians Begin Advance on Bulgars—Thousands of Prisoners Taken—Surrender of Bulgaria—Panic in Berlin—Passage Through the Country Granted for Armies of the Allies—Ferdinand Abdicates—Germany's Imagined Mittel-Europa Dream Forever Destroyed 154

CONTENTS

CHAPTER X. THE CENTRAL EMPIRES WHINE FOR PEACE
Austria-Hungary Makes the First Plea—President Wilson's Abrupt Answer—Prince Max Camouflaged as an Apostle of Peace made Chancellor and Opens Germany's Pathetic Plea for a Peace by Negotiation—The President Replies on Behalf of all the Allied Powers—Foch Pushes on Regardless of Peace Notes 175

CHAPTER XI. BATTLES IN THE AIR
Conquering the Fear of Death—From Individual Fights to Battles Between Squadrons—Heroes of the Warring Nations—America's Wonderful Record—From Nowhere to First Place in Eighteen Months—The Liberty Motor 191

CHAPTER XII. HEALTH AND HAPPINESS OF THE AMERICAN FORCES
Record of the Red Cross on all Fronts—A Gigantic Work Well Executed—Y. M. C. A.—Y. W. C. A.—Knights of Columbus—Jewish Welfare Association—Salvation Army—American Library Association—Other Organizations—Surgery and Sanitation 210

ILLUSTRATIONS

VOLUME V

	PAGE
JERUSALEM DELIVERED	*Frontispiece*
THE FIRST OF THE TIDAL WAVE OF KHAKI	22
THE LARGEST SHIP IN THE WORLD AS A U. S. TRANSPORT	26
THE GREATEST SHIPYARD IN THE WORLD	34
THE GERMAN GENERAL STAFF	70
AMERICA GETS INTO THE WAR AT CANTIGNY	74
CHÂTEAU-THIERRY, WHERE AMERICA INFLICTED A SECOND GETTYSBURG ON GERMANY	82
WIPING OUT THE ST. MIHIEL SALIENT	86
FAMOUS BRITISH GENERALS	114
STORMING THE MOLE AT ZEEBRUGGE	126
BELGIAN SOVEREIGNS RE-ENTER BRUGES	136
THE FIRST DAY ON THE PIAVE	146
AMERICAN TROOPS ON THE ITALIAN FRONT	148
PICKING ONE "OFF THE TAIL"	194
THE Y. M. C. A. IN THE FRONT LINE TRENCHES	216

THE WORLD WAR

CHAPTER I

REDEMPTION OF THE HOLY LAND

FROM the beginning of the war the German General Staff and the British War Office planned the occupation of Palestine and Macedonia. Germany wanted domination of that territory because through it lay the open road to Egypt and British prestige in the East. Turkey was the cat's paw of the Hun in this enterprise. German officers and German guns were supplied to the Turks, but the terrible privations necessary in a long campaign that must be spent largely in the desert, and the inevitable great loss in human life, were both demanded from Turkey.

Great Britain made no such demands upon any of its Allies. Unflinchingly England faced virtually alone the rigors, the disease and the deaths consequent upon an expedition having as its object the redemption of the Holy Land from the unspeakable Turk.

Volunteers for the expedition came by the thousands. Canada, the United States, Australia and other countries furnished whole regiments of Jewish youths eager for the campaign. The inspiration and the devotion radiating from Palestine, and particularly from Jerusalem and Bethlehem, drew Jew and Gentile, hardy adventurer and zealous churchman, into Allenby's great army.

It was a long campaign. On February 26, 1917, Kut-el-Amara was recaptured from the Turks by the British expedition under command of General Sir Stanley Maude, and on March 11th following General Maude captured Bagdad. From that time forward pressure upon the Turks was continuous. On September 29, 1917, the Turkish Mesopotamian army commanded by Ahmed Bey was routed by the British, and historic Beersheba in Palestine was occupied on October 31st. The untimely death of General Maude, the hero of

THE HOLY LAND

Mesopotamia, on November 18th, 1917, temporarily cast gloom over the Allied forces but it had no deterrent effect upon their successful operations. Siege was laid to Jerusalem and its environs late in November, and on December 8, 1917, the Holy City which had been held by the Turks for six hundred and seventy-three years surrendered to General Allenby and his British army. Thus ended a struggle for possession of the holiest of shrines both of the Old and New Testaments, that had cost millions of lives during fruitless crusades and had been the center of religious aspirations for ages.

General Allenby's official report follows:

"I entered the city officially at noon December 11th with a few of my staff, the commanders of the French and Italian detachments, the heads of the political missions, and the military attachés of France, England, and America.

"The procession was all afoot, and at Jaffa gate I was received by the guards representing England, Scotland, Ireland, Wales, Australia, New Zealand, India, France and Italy. The population received me well.

4 THE WORLD WAR

"Guards have been placed over the holy places. My military governor is in contact

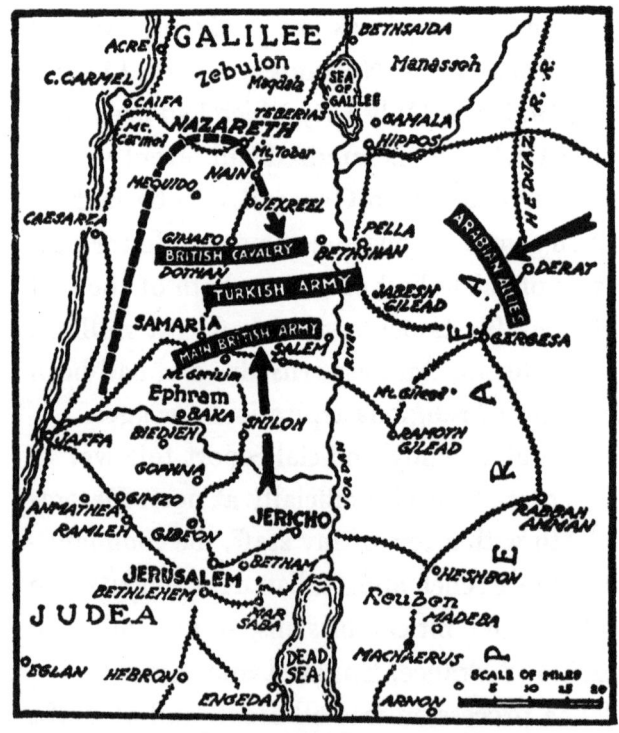

How the British Army Trapped the Turks

with the acting custodians and the Latin and Greek representatives. The governor has detailed an officer to supervise the holy places.

THE HOLY LAND

The Mosque of Omar and the area around it have been placed under Moslem control, and a military cordon of Mohammedan officers and soldiers has been established around the mosque. Orders have been issued that no non-Moslem is to pass within the cordon without permission of the military governor and the Moslem in charge."

A proclamation in Arabic, Hebrew, English, French, Italian, Greek and Russian was posted in the citadel, and on all the walls proclaiming martial law and intimating that all the holy places would be maintained and protected according to the customs and beliefs of those to whose faith they were sacred. The proclamation read:

PROCLAMATION

To the Inhabitants of Jerusalem the Blessed and the People Dwelling in Its Vicinity.

The defeat inflicted upon the Turks by the troops under my command has resulted in the occupation of your city by my forces. I, therefore, proclaim it to be under martial law, under which form of administration it will remain so long as military consideration makes necessary.

However, lest any of you be alarmed by reason of

your experience at the hands of the enemy who has retired, I hereby inform you that it is my desire that every person should pursue his lawful business without fear of interruption.

Furthermore, since your city is regarded with affection by the adherents of three of the great religions of mankind and its soil has been consecrated by the prayers and pilgrimages of multitudes of devout people of these three religions for many centuries, therefore, do I make it known to you that every sacred building, monument, holy spot, shrine, traditional site, endowment, pious bequest, or customary place of prayer of whatsoever form of the three religions will be maintained and protected according to the existing customs and beliefs of those to whose faith they are sacred.

Guardians have been established at Bethlehem and on Rachel's Tomb. The tomb at Hebron has been placed under exclusive Moslem control.

The hereditary custodians at the gates of the Holy Sepulchre have been requested to take up their accustomed duties in remembrance of the magnanimous act of the Caliph Omar, who protected that church.

Jerusalem was now made the center of the British operations against the Turks in Palestine. Mohammed V, the Sultan of Turkey, died July 3, 1918, and many superstitious Turks looked upon that event as forecasting the end of the Turkish Empire. The Turkish army in Palestine was left largely to its fate by

THE HOLY LAND

Germany and Austria, and although it was numerically a formidable opponent for General Allenby's forces, that distinguished strategist fairly outmaneuvered the Turkish High Command in every encounter. The beginning of the end for Turkish misrule in Palestine came on September 20th when the ancient town of Nazareth was captured by the British.

A military net was thereupon closed upon the Turkish army. The fortified towns of Beisan and Afule followed the fate of Nazareth. In one day's fighting 18,000 Turkish prisoners, 120 guns, four airplanes, a number of locomotives and cars, and a great quantity of military and food supplies were bagged by the victorious British. So well did Allenby plan that the British losses were far the smallest suffered in any large operation of the entire war. It was the swiftest and most decisive victory of any scored by the Allies. It ended the grandiose dream of Germany for an invasion of Egypt in stark disaster, and swept the Holy Land clear of the Turks.

This great battle on the Biblical field of

Armageddon was remarkable in that it was virtually the only engagement during the entire war offering the freest scope to cavalry operations. British cavalry commands operated over a radius of sixty miles between the Jordan and the Mediterranean, sweeping the Turks before them.

By September 25th the total bag of Turkish prisoners exceeded 40,000. Munition depots covering acres of ground were taken. Whole companies of Turkish soldiers were found sitting on their white flags waiting for the British to accept their terms. Two hundred sixty-five pieces of artillery were captured.

Damascus was captured on Tuesday, October 1st after an advance of 130 miles by General Allenby since September 1st the day of his surprise attack north of Jerusalem. During that period a total of 73,000 prisoners was captured.

Palestine's delivery from the Turks was complete. Official announcement was made by the British War Office that the total casualties from all sources in this final campaign was less than 4,000.

Plans for the government of the people of Palestine were announced immediately. Their general scope was outlined in an agreement made between the British, French and Russian governments in 1916. Under that arrangement Republican France was charged with the preparation of a scheme of self-government. The town of Alexandretta was fixed upon as a free port of entry for the new nation.

CHAPTER II

Transportation Problems

WHEN America entered the war there was a very great increase in the volume of business of the railroads of the country. The roads were already so crowded by what the Allies had done in purchasing war supplies, that a great deal of confusion had resulted. The Allies had expended more than three billion dollars in the United States and as nearly all of their purchases had to be sent to a few definite points for shipment to Europe, the congestion at those points had become a serious difficulty. Thousands of loaded cars had to stand for long periods awaiting the transfer of their contents to ships. This meant that thousands of cars which had been taken from lines in other parts of the country would be in a traffic blockade for weeks at a time. The main dif-

TRANSPORTATION 11

ficulty appeared to be that of getting trains unloaded promptly.

The declaration of war by the United States made the situation very much worse. Not only did the railroads have to handle the freight destined for the Allies, but there was a very large addition to the passenger movement on account of the thousands of men that were being sent to the various training camps, and the immense masses of supplies that had to be sent to these camps. This included not only the ordinary supplies to the men but thousands of carloads of lumber. Moreover, all over the country mills and factories were now being handed over to the government for war work; and to them, too, great quantities of raw material had to be sent, and the finished product removed to its destination.

A vigorous endeavor to meet the new difficulties was instituted by the railroads themselves. They themselves named a war board, which was to co-operate with the government and which was to have absolute authority. But this arrangement soon proved unsatisfactory. Each government official would do his best to obtain preference for what his department required, and to obtain that preference a system of priority tags was established which became a great abuse. The result was that priority freight soon began to crowd out the freight which the railroads could handle according to their own discretion, thus seriously interfering with business all over the country.

Naturally, the railroad executives and the government authorities studied the question with the greatest care, but they could not reach an understanding among themselves, nor with the Administration. At last the President settled the matter by announcing his decision to have the government take over complete control of the roads. The President derived his power from an Act of Congress dated August 29, 1916, which reads as follows:

> The President in time of war is empowered, through the Secretary of War, to take possession and assume control of any system or systems of transportation, or any part thereof, and to utilize the same to the exclusion, as far as may be necessary, of all other traffic thereon, for the transfer or transportation of troops, war ma-

TRANSPORTATION

terial and equipment, or for such other purposes connected with the emergency as may be needful or desirable.

The proclamation went into effect on December 28, 1917, and the President declared that it applied to "each and every system of transportation and the appurtenances thereof, located, wholly or in part, within the boundaries of the Continental United States, and consisting of railroads and owned or controlled systems of coastwise and inland transportation, engaged in general transportation, whether operated by steam, or by electric power, including also terminals, terminal companies, and terminal associations, sleeping and parlor cars, private cars, and private car lines, elevators, warehouses, telegraph and telephone lines, and all other equipment and appurtenances commonly used upon or operated as a part of such rail or combined rail and water systems of transportation. . . . That the possession, control, operation, and utilization of such transportation systems shall be exercised by and through William G. McAdoo, who is hereby appointed, and designated Director General of Railroads. Said Director may perform the duties imposed upon him so long and to such an extent as he shall determine through the boards of directors, receivers, officers and employees, of said system of transportation." President Wilson issued an explanation with this proclamation in which he said:

> This is a war of resources no less than of men, perhaps even more than of men, and it is necessary for the complete mobilization of our resources that the transportation systems of the country should be organized and employed under a single authority and to simplify methods for co-ordination which have not proved possible under private management and control. A committee of railway executives who have been co-operating with the government in this all-important matter, have done the utmost that it was possible for them to do, but there were differences that they could neither escape nor neutralize. Complete unity of administration in the present circumstances involves upon occasion, and at many points, a serious dislocation of earnings, and the committee was, of course, without power or authority to rearrange charges or effect proper compensations in adjustments of earnings. Several roads which were willingly and with admirable public spirit accepting the orders of the committee, have already suffered from

TRANSPORTATION 15

these circumstances, and should not be required to suffer further. In mere fairness to them, the full authority of the government must be substituted. The public interest must be first served, and in addition the financial interests of the government, and the financial interests of the railways must be brought under a common direction. The financial operations of the railway need not, then, interfere with the borrowings of the government, and they themselves can be conducted at a great advantage. Investors in railway securities may rest assured that their rights and interests will be as scrupulously looked after by the government as they could be by the directors of the several railway systems. Immediately upon the reassembling of Congress I shall recommend that these different guarantees be given. The Secretary of War and I are agreed that, all the circumstances being taken into consideration, the best results can be obtained under the immediate executive direction of the Honorable William G. McAdoo, whose practical experience peculiarly fits him for the service, and whose authority as Secretary of the Treasurer will enable him to co-ordinate, as no other man could, the many financial interests which will be involved, and which might, unless systematically directed, suffer very embarrassing entanglements.

President Wilson's proclamation stirred up great excitement on the stock market. Speculators rushed to buy back railroad stocks which they had previously sold short, and the market value of such stocks was raised more than three hundred and fifty million dollars as a result. The Federal Government's assumption of control of the railroads was generally recognized as the proper act under existing circumstances, and the guarantee of pre-war earnings made them a good investment.

The railroad system in the United States consists of 260,000 miles of railroad, owned by 41 distinct corporations, with about 650,000 shareholders. It employs 1,600,000 men and represents a property investment of $17,500,000,000. The outstanding capital in round numbers is $16,000,000,000, $9,000,000,000 of which is represented by a funded debt. The rolling stock comprises 61,000 locomotives, 2,250,000 freight cars, 52,000 passenger cars and 95,000 service cars. All this was now under the charge of William G. McAdoo. On January 4, 1918, President Wilson explained his plan to Congress, and recommended legislation to put the new system of control into effect, and to guarantee to the holders of railroad stocks and bonds a net annual income equal to the average net income for the three years ending June 30, 1917.

The wise recommendations of President Wilson were at once approved by Congress; provision was made for guaranteeing the railroads the income which he recommended, and for financing the roads. The railroads' war board was abolished and Mr. McAdoo appointed an advisory board to assist him. This board consisted of John Skelton Williams, Controller of the Currency; Hale Holden, President of the Chicago, Burlington and Quincy Railroad; Henry Walters, Chairman of the Board of Directors of the Atlantic Coast Line; Edward Chambers, Vice-President of the Santa Fé Railroad and head of the transportation division of the United States Food Administration; Walter D. Hines, Chairman of the Executive Committee of the Santa Fé. Specific duties were assigned to the various members of this committee. Mr. Williams was to deal with the financial problem; Mr. Holden to assume direction of committees and sub-committees, and other phases of the work were allotted to other members. Mr. Walter D. Hines was made assistant to the Director General.

Mr. McAdoo's first order was to pool all terminals, ports, locomotives, rolling stock and other transportation facilities. Another order had as its object to end the congestion of traffic in New York City and Chicago. It gave all lines entering these centers equal rights in trackage and water terminal facilities. This wiped out the identity of the great Pennsylvania Terminal Station in New York, and gave all railroads the use of the Pennsylvania tubes under the Hudson River.

The effect of government control of the railroads was felt from the very first. Coal was given the right of way, giving great relief to such sections as were suffering from fuel shortage. Many passenger trains were taken off, more than two hundred and fifty of such trains being dropped from the schedules of the eastern roads. This permitted a great increase in the freight traffic. Orders were also given that all empty

TRANSPORTATION

box cars were to be sent to wheat-producing centers, so that wheat could be moved to the Atlantic sea coasts for shipment to England and France. These orders preceded the adoption of the railroad control bill, which was not passed by Congress until March 14th. A feature of the bill is the proviso that government control of the railroads shall not continue more than twenty-one months after the war. After the passing of the bill plans were made to make contracts with each railroad company for government compensation on the basis provided in the bill.

The action of the government in thus assuming control of the railroads very naturally led to wide differences of opinion, some of which were sharply expressed in the Congress of the United States. On the whole, however, public opinion decided that the government acted wisely. Certain inconveniences to the traveling public were easily excused when it was realized that the movement of troops throughout the country to the camps, or from the camps to the ports which were to take them across the sea, from "Texas to Toul," was being accomplished with great success; that the movement of war material was now possible, and that the gigantic railroad system was working without a hitch.

Many details, in connection with the railroad management, were not at once worked out, and many months passed without complete agreements regarding the railway operating contracts. But this was a matter of greater interest to the owners than it was to patriotic citizens, anxious for the winning of the war. Governmental control of the railroads was only a beginning. On July 16th President Wilson took control, for the period of the war, of all telegraph, telephone, cable and radio lines, signing a bill on that day passed by Congress authorizing such action.

The transportation of the American army across the ocean was the greatest military feat of its kind ever accomplished in history. The transportation of English troops during the Boer War meant a longer journey, but the

TRANSPORTATION

number of troops sent on that journey was but a small fraction of America's army.

The railroads in existence were not sufficient. The ships that were necessary could not be found in America's navy. It was necessary to build new roads, new docks, new terminals, new bases of supplies in America, and to send abroad thousands of trained workmen and experienced railroad engineers to build similar necessities in France. To convey the millions of men across the water England had to come to the rescue, and though hundreds of American ships were built with a speed that was almost miraculous, they were in constant need of the assistance of the Allies. But wonderful men were put in charge of the work, wonderful organizers with wonderful assistants, and the great task was accomplished.

As soon as the army was trained it was sent across—first by thousands, then by tens of thousands, then by hundreds of thousands, until before the war was over more than two million men had made the great trip "over there." And throughout that whole trip they were watched over as carefully as if they were at home. Every want was supplied; food, clothing, munitions were all where they were needed. Even their leisure hours were looked after, their health attended to. Books, games, theaters, study classes, all were there.

It was a wonderful performance, and the whole movement was conducted with clock-like precision. On such a day at such an hour the trained soldier would start. At such an hour he would report in some Atlantic port. At such an hour and such a minute he would board ship, and with equal precision that ship would sail upon the appointed moment. Perhaps on the journey over some submarine might delay the ship, but the destroyers were there on the alert, and the submarine was but an amusing episode. On the other side the process was carried on with equal efficiency. Before the American doughboy could realize that he was in France he was in his quarters, just like home, in the base camps behind the fighting line, and it was this miracle of transportation that won the war.

THE FIRST OF THE TIDAL WAVE OF KHAKI

Beginning with the handful of American soldiers who landed in France on June 8, 1917, the flood of troops poured the "bridge of ships" in ever increasing volume until at the end of the war nearly two million soldiers had been transported to France

CHAPTER III

SHIPS AND THE MEN WHO MADE THEM

WHEN the United States of America entered the World War she was confronted at once by a serious question. The great Allied nations were struggling against the attempt of the Germans, through the piratical use of submarines, to blockade the coast of the Allied countries. It was this German action which had led America to take part in the war. It is true that America had other motives. Few wars ever take place among democratic nations as a result of the calculation of the nation's leaders. The people must be interested, and the people must sympathize with the cause for which they are going to fight. The people of America had sympathized with Belgium, and had become indignant at the brutal treatment of that inoffensive nation. They had sympathized with

France in its gallant endeavor to protect its soil from the inroads of the Hun. This feeling had become a personal one as they reviewed the lists of Americans lost in the sinking of the Lusitania, and this sympathy had gradually grown into indignation when the Germans, after having promised to conduct submarine warfare according to international law, again and again violated that promise. When, then, the Germans declared that they would no longer even pretend to treat neutral shipping according to the laws of maritime warfare the people with one accord approved the action of the President of the United States in declaring war. The Germans at this time were making a desperate effort to starve England, by destroying its commerce, and it was in the endeavor to accomplish this purpose that they thought it necessary to attack American ships.

The first effort of Americans, therefore, was naturally to use every power of the navy to destroy the lurking submarines, and in the second place to use every means in their power to supply the Allies with food. But America had for many years neglected to give encouragement to her merchant fleets. Her commerce was very largely carried in foreign bottoms.

Ships were needed, and needed urgently, and one of the very first acts of the American Government was to authorize their production. Congress therefore appropriated for this purpose what was then the extraordinary sum of $1,135,000,000 and General Goethals, recently returned from his work in building the Panama Canal, was appointed manager of the Emergency Fleet Corporation and entrusted with the execution of the government's shipbuilding program.

The Emergency Fleet Corporation, however, was then independent of the United States Shipping Board, of which Mr. William Denman was made chairman, and friction between General Goethals and Mr. Denman at the very start caused long delay. The difference of opinion between them arose over the comparative merits of wooden and steel ships. The matter was finally laid before President

Wilson and ended in the resignation of both men and the complete reorganization of the board and the Fleet Corporation, in which reorganization the Fleet Corporation was made subordinate to the Shipping Board but given entire control of construction.

Rear-Admiral Capps succeeded General Goethals, but was compelled to resign on account of ill health. Rear-Admiral Harris, who had been chief of the Navy's Bureau of Yards and Docks, then had the job for two weeks, but resigned because in his opinion he had not enough authority. Then came Mr. Charles Piez, who held the position for a longer period. Mr. Edward N. Hurley had been made chairman of the United States Shipping Board, and under the direction of these two men much progress was made.

In the spring of 1918 the boards themselves were not satisfied with their progress, and on April 16, 1918, Mr. Charles M. Schwab, chairman of the Board of Directors of the Bethlehem Steel Corporation, was made Director General of the Emergency Fleet Corpora-

THE LARGEST SHIP IN THE WORLD AS A U. S. TRANSPORT

Among the German ships taken over by the United States at the outbreak of the war was the "Vaterland," the largest ship ever built. She was renamed the "Leviathan" and used as a transport, carrying 12,000 American soldiers across the ocean on each trip. She is shown here entering a French harbor at the end of a successful passage.

SHIPS AND THE MEN 27

tion. Mr. Schwab was one of the most prominent business men in the United States and one of the best known, and his appointment was received all over the country with the greatest satisfaction. His wonderful work in building up the Bethlehem steel plant not only showed his great ability, but especially fitted him for a task in which the steel industry bore such a vital part. The official statement issued from the White House read as follows:

Edward N. Hurley, Charles M. Schwab, Bainbridge Colby and Charles Piez were received by the President at the White House today. It was stated that the subject discussed was the progress and condition of a national ship-building program. The carrying forward of the construction work in the one hundred and thirty shipyards now in operation is so vast that it requires a reinforcement of the ship-building organization throughout the country. Later in the day Chairman Hurley of the Shipping Board announced that a new office with wide powers had been created by the Trustees of the Emergency Fleet Corporation. The new position is that of Director General and Mr. Schwab has been asked, and has agreed, to accept this position in answer to the call of the nation. Charles Piez, Vice-President of the Emergency Fleet Corporation, recommended that the post of General Manager of the corporation be at once abolished, so that Mr. Schwab as Director General should be wholly unhampered in carrying on the large task entrusted to him. Mr. Piez, since the retirement of Admiral Harris, has been filling both the position of Vice-President and that of General Manager. Mr. Schwab will have complete supervision and direction of the work of ship-building. He agreed to take up the work at the sacrifice of his personal wishes in the matter. His services were virtually commandeered. His great experience as a steel maker and builder of ships has been drafted for the nation.

Although the fact that production during the month of March had not been as great as had been hoped probably brought about this change, it should also be said that those who had been responsible deserved much credit for what had actually been done. They had been handicapped constantly by poor transportation and shortage of materials, but had worked faithfully and with what under ordinary circumstances would be regarded as remarkable success. The call upon Mr. Schwab was simply an effort to draft into the service of the country its very highest executive ability. Mr. Schwab's name had been mentioned before for more than one government post, and it was thought that here was the place where his talents could have the fullest play. It was stated in Washington that he would receive a salary of one dollar a year.

Mr. Schwab at once proceeded to "speed up" the shipping program. It took him just one day to arrange his own business affairs and then he began his work. His first day was spent in going over the details of his task with Chairman Hurley and Mr. Piez. He then received newspaper men, beginning the campaign of publicity which turned out to be so successful. He was full of compliments for the work which had already been done. "It is prodigious, splendid, magnificent!" he said. "It is far greater than any man who hasn't seen the inside of things can appreciate. The foundation is laid. That task is well done. We are going to get the results which are needed and I should be proud if I could have any part in the accomplishment. All I can say for myself is that I am filled with enthusiasm, energy and confidence. Mr. Hurley and I are in full accord on everything, and we are going to work shoulder to shoulder to make the work a success, but the large burden must fall upon the people at the yards, and they are entitled to any credit for success. I do not want to have any man in the shipyards working for me. I want them all working with me. Nothing is going to be worth while unless we win this war, and every one must do the task to which he is called."

One of the first steps that Mr. Schwab took to speed up ship production was to establish his headquarters in Philadelphia, as the center of the ship-building region. Chairman Hurley remained at Washington, and the operating department, which included agencies such as the Inter-Allied Ship Control Committee, was removed to New York City. It was stated that nearly fifty per cent of the work in progress was within a short radius of Philadelphia.

The year before the war the total output of the United States shipyards was only two hundred and fifty thousand tons. The program of the shipping board contemplated the construction of one thousand one hundred and forty-five steel ships, with a tonnage of eight million, one

SHIPS AND THE MEN 31

hundred and sixty-four thousand, five hundred and eight, and four hundred and ninety wooden ships, with a tonnage of one million seven hundred and fifteen thousand. These of course could not be built in the shipyards then in existence. New shipyards had to be built in various parts of the country.

In the first year after the shipping board took control, one hundred and eighty-eight ships were put in the water and through requisition and by building, one hundred and three more were added to the American merchant fleet. By April, 1918, the government had at its service 2,762,605 tons of shipping. During the month of May, the first month after Mr. Schwab began his work, the record of production had mounted from 160,286 tons to 263,571. American shipyards had completed and delivered during that month forty-three steel ships and one wooden ship. Mr. Hurley, in an address on June 10th, said:

> On June 1st, we had increased the American built tonnage to over 3,500,000 dead-weight tons of shipping. This gives us a total of more than one thousand four

hundred ships with an approximate total dead-weight tonnage of 7,000,000 now under the control of the United States Shipping Board. In round numbers and from all sources we have added to the American flag since our war against Germany began, nearly 4,500,000 tons of shipping. Our program calls for the building of 1,856 passenger, cargo and refrigerator ships and tankers, ranging from five thousand to twelve thousand tons each, with an aggregate dead-weight of thirteen million. Exclusive of these we have two hundred and forty-five commandeered vessels, taken over from foreign and domestic owners which are being completed by the Emergency Fleet Corporation. These will aggregate a total dead-weight tonnage of 1,715,000. This makes a total of two thousand one hundred and one vessels, exclusive of tugs and barges which are being built and will be put on the seas in the course of carrying out the present program, with an aggregate dead-weight tonnage of 14,715,000. Five billion dollars will be required to finish our program, but the expenditure of this enormous sum will give to the American people the greatest merchant fleet ever assembled in the history of the world. American workmen have made the expansion of recent months possible, and they will make possible the successful conclusion of the whole program.

In the wonderful work that followed his appointment Mr. Schwab constantly came before the public, mainly through his addresses to the working men of the different yards. His main endeavor was to stimulate enthusiasm and rivalry among the men. A ten-thousand-dollar prize was offered to the yard producing the largest surplus above its program, and he traveled throughout the country urging the employees at all the great yards to break their records. The result of his work was that it was not long before it was announced that the monthly tonnage of ships completed by the Allies exceeded the tonnage of those sunk by the German submarine. The menace of the submarine which had seemed so formidable, had disappeared.

The most important of the great shipyards which were producing the American cargo ships was at Hog Island in the southwest part of Philadelphia. This shipyard may indeed be called the greatest shipyard in the world. Before Mr. Schwab became Director General much criticism had been launched at the work that was going on there, and an investigation had been made which resulted in a favorable report. On August 5th the new shipyard launched its first ship, the 7,500 ton freight steamer, Quistconck, in the presence of a distinguished throng among whom were the President of the United States and Mrs. Woodrow Wilson. The ship was christened by Mrs. Wilson, and the President swung his hat and led the cheers as the great ship glided down the ways. The name "Quistconck" is the ancient Indian name of Hog Island. The crowd numbered more than sixty thousand people, and special trains from Washington and New York brought many notable guests. President and Mrs. Wilson were escorted by Mr. Hurley and Mr. Schwab, and apparently thoroughly enjoyed the occasion. An enormous bouquet was presented to Mrs. Wilson by Foreman McMillan, who had driven the first rivet in the Quistconck's keel.

Shortly after the armistice it was announced the Hog Island plant would be acquired by the United States Government. The real estate, valued at $1,760,000, was owned by the American International Ship Building Company, and the government had invested about $60,000,000 in equipping the plant. At the time the war ended thirty-five thousand per-

THE GREATEST SHIPYARD IN THE WORLD

View of Hog Island shipyard near Philadelphia, showing the forest of derricks rising from its fifty shipways. At the time the war ended, 35,000 persons were at work and 180 ships were in course of completion.

sons were at work and a hundred and eighty ships were in various stages of completion.

An interesting feature in connection with the endeavor to "speed up" was the competition in riveting. Early in the year in yard after yard expert riveters were reported as making extraordinary records, and prizes were offered to the winners of such records. Later, however, such contests were discouraged by Chairman Hurley and by others. The best record was made by John Omir, who drove twelve thousand two hundred and nine rivets in nine hours at the Belfast Yards of Workman and Clark. In the accomplishment of this feat on two occasions he passed the mark of one thousand four hundred rivets an hour. In his best minute he drove twenty-six rivets.

The ships constructed by the Shipping Board were of steel, of wood and of concrete, and at times considerable difference of opinion existed with regard to which form of ship should receive the most attention. The policy of the government seemed finally to favor the steel as it was claimed that the wooden type was not only more expensive, but that it was less efficient. However until the very end wooden ships in great numbers were being built.

On May 31st the steamship Agawam, described as the first fabricated ship in the world, was launched in the yards of the Submarine Boat Corporation at Newark. This was essentially a standardized steel cargo ship. "Fabricated" is the technical term applied to ships built from numbered shapes made from patterns.

President Carse, of the Submarine Boat Corporation, said that the Agawam was the first of a hundred and fifty vessels of that type which would be constructed in the yard. The parts were made, he said, in bridge and tank shops throughout the country and were assembled at the yard. "Ninety-five per cent of the work in forming the parts entering into the hull of this vessel, and punching rivet holes, is done at shops widely separated, from drawings furnished by this company, and these drawings have been of such exactitude, and the work has been so carefully performed by the different bridge shops that when they are brought together at this yard they fit perfectly and the ship as you see is absolutely fair. The construction of the hull of this vessel requires the driving of over four hundred thousand rivets, and by our method more than one quarter of these rivets are driven at the distant shops, the different parts being brought to the yard in sections as large as can be transported on the railroad. Each part is numbered and lettered and as they are shaped perfectly all that is necessary is to place them in position, bolt them, and finally fasten them with rivets."

Officials of the company said that they expected to launch in the course of time two such vessels in each week. A standard ship of this type has a dead weight carrying capacity of five thousand five hundred tons. It is three hundred and forty-three feet long and forty-six feet wide and is expected to show an average speed of ten and a half knots. Fuel oil is used to generate steam, to drive a turbine operating three thousand six hundred revolutions a minute. The oil is carried in compartments of the double bottom of the ship in sufficient quantity for more than a round trip to Europe. Twenty-seven steel mills, fifty-six fabricating plants, and two hundred foundries and equipment shops were drawn upon to construct the ship.

In addition to the steel and wood vessels the Emergency Fleet Corporation also constructed a number of concrete ships. The first step in this direction was taken on April 3rd, when the construction of four 7,500 ton concrete ships at a Pacific coast shipyard was authorized. This action was taken as a result of a report on the trials made with the concrete ship, Faith, which was built in San Francisco by private capital. The test of this ship had been satisfactory and Mr. R. J. Wig, an agent of the Emergency Fleet Corporation, who had made a careful inspection of the Faith and watched the tests, reported his confidence in the new cargo carrier. The successful trial trip of the Faith led, on the 17th of May, to the government order that fifty-eight more such ships be constructed. Sites for yards were leased and contracts awarded. The concrete ship turned out to be a great success.

The extraordinary success of the American ship-building program during the World War was due to the enthusiasm of the workmen employed at the government plants, and that same enthusiasm was found in connection with their work in every industry on which the Government made demands. American labor was thoroughly loyal. It recognized that in the war for democracy against autocracy it had a vital concern. The attitude of the great American labor unions must however be sharply distinguished from that of the extreme socialists who refused to take any part in helping to win the war.

From the very beginning, the American Federation of Labor took a patriotic stand. Its leader was Mr. Samuel Gompers, and it was fortunate for America that the leadership of this great organization was in such patriotic hands. Mr. Gompers had been for many years president of this great labor organization, and was so often called in consultation by the President of the United States in connection with labor affairs that he might almost be called an unofficial member of the President's cabinet. Mr. Gompers was by birth an Englishman, but he had left his home when still a boy and was thoroughly filled with true American patriotism. From the beginning he devoted himself with the greatest enthusiasm not only to the protection of the interests of which he was in charge, but to the prosecution of a successful war. He had to contend, as labor leaders in other countries had been compelled to contend, with socialistic and anarchistic organizations.

During the period of America's participation in the war there were certain disturbances caused by the I. W. W., but from such movements the American Federation of Labor held itself aloof. Occasional strikes, on account of special conditions, were easily settled. The governmental assumption of control over railroads and other essential industries had much to do with the peaceful attitude of the workmen. The very high wages which were offered to the workmen at munitions works, shipbuilding plants and other governmental enterprises enabled the workmen there to live in reasonable comfort, though it caused a great deal of trouble in private industry, and compelled an increase in pay to labor all over the land.

In the latter part of the war Mr. Gompers traveled abroad, as a representative of American labor, and was greeted everywhere with the utmost enthusiasm, while his influence was strongly felt in favor of moderate and sane views as to labor's rights.

The American situation with regard to labor was made much simpler by the organization of the United States Employment Service. This was made an arm of the Department of Labor, with branch offices in nearly all the large cities of every State. It had a large corps of traveling examiners, men skilled in determining the fitness of workers for particular jobs, and it undertook to recruit labor for the various war industries in which they were needed. During the last year of the war from a hundred and fifty thousand to two hundred thousand workers of all kinds were given work each month. In addition to this the Employment Service was a clearing house of information for manufacturers. The Director General of this service was Mr. John B. Densmore.

Labor throughout the country, except when influenced by men of foreign birth who were not in touch with the spirit of America, was universally loyal, and its share in the winning of the war will always remain a matter for pride.

CHAPTER IV

GERMANY'S DYING DESPERATE EFFORT

IN the spring of 1918 it must have been plain to the German High Command that if the war was to be won it must be won at once. In spite of all their leaders said of the impossibility of bringing an American army to France they must have been well informed of what the Americans were doing. They knew that there were already more than two million men in active training in the American army, and while at that time only a small proportion of them were available on the battle front, yet every day that proportion was growing greater and by the middle of the summer the little American army would have become a tremendous fighting force.

Their own armies on their western front had been enormously increased in size by the removal to that front of troops from Russia.

Hundreds of thousands of their best regiments were now withdrawn from the east and incorporated under the command of their great Generals, Hindenburg and Ludendorff, in the armies of the west. They must, therefore, take advantage of this increased force and win the war before the Americans could come.

The problem of the Allies was also simple. It was not necessary for them to plan a great offensive. All they had to do was to hold out until, through the American aid which was coming now in such numbers, their armies would be so increased that German resistance would be futile. Under such circumstances began the last great offensive of the German army.

At that time it seems probable that the armies of Great Britain and France numbered about three million, five hundred thousand men, and that, of these, six hundred and seventy thousand were on the front lines when the German attack began leaving an army of reserve of about two million, eight hundred and fifty thousand men. A considerable

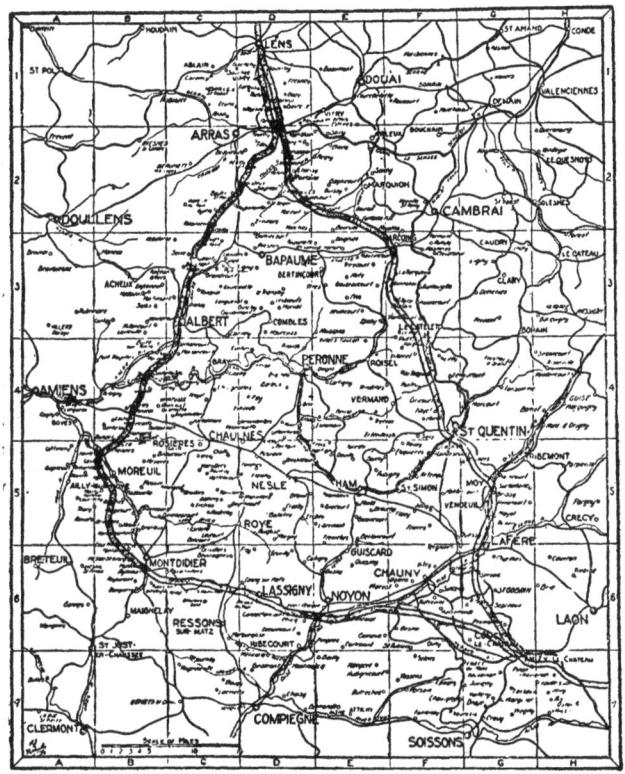

HOW GERMANY ATTEMPTED TO DIVIDE THE ALLIED ARMIES

The map shows the ground covered by the Germans in the terrific Picardy drive of March, 1918, which had for its object the capture of Amiens and the push forward along the Somme to the channel, thus dividing the British army in the north from the French and Americans in the south.

number of these were probably in England on leave. The number of French soldiers must have been between four and five million, of whom about one million five hundred thousand were on the front line. Adding to these the American, Belgian, Portuguese, Russian and Polish troops the Allied forces could not have been short of eight million, five hundred thousand men.

The strength of the Germans on the Western front before the Russian Revolution was probably about four million, five hundred thousand men, and the withdrawal of Russia from the war had added to that number probably as many as one million, five hundred thousand men, making an army of six million men to oppose that of the Allies. The Allies, therefore, must have considerably outnumbered the Germans.

In spite of this fact in nearly all the engagements in the early part of the great offensive the Allied forces were outnumbered in a ratio varying from three to one to five to three. This was possible, first, because in any offen-

GERMANY'S LAST EFFORT 47

sive the attacking side naturally concentrates as many troops as it can gather at the point from which the offense is to begin, and second, since the Allies were not under one command it was with great difficulty that arrangements could be made by which the forces of one nation could reinforce the armies of another.

The first difficulty of course could not be obviated, but the solution of the second difficulty was the appointment of General Foch as Commander-in-Chief of all the Allied forces.

The appointment was made on March 28th and all the influence of the United States had been exerted in its favor. General Pershing at once offered to General Foch the unrestricted use of the American force in France and it was agreed that a large part of the American army should be brigaded with the Allied troops wherever there were weak spots.

Foch was already famous as the greatest strategist in Europe. He comes of a Basque family and was born in the town of Tarbes, in the Department of the Hautes-Pyrenees, which is on the border of Spain, on October

2, 1851. Foch served as a subaltern in the Franco-Prussian War and at twenty-six was made Captain in the artillery. Later he became Professor of Tactics in the Ecole de Guerre, where he remained for five years. He then returned to regimental work and won steady promotion until he became Brigadier-General. He was sent back to the War College as Director and wrote two books, "The Principles of War" and "Conduct of War," which have been translated into English, German and Italian and are considered standard works. He was now recognized as a man of unusual ability and was appointed to the command first, of the Thirteenth division, then of the Eighth corps at Bourges, and then to the command of the Twentieth corps at Nancy.

Unlike Marshal Joffre who was cool, careful, slow moving, Marshal Foch is full of daring and impetuosity. Everything is calculated scientifically but his strategy is full of dash. Many of his sayings have been passed from mouth to mouth among the Allies.

"Find out the weak point of your enemy and deliver your blow there," he said once at a staff banquet.

"But suppose, General," said an officer, "that the enemy has no weak point?"

"If the enemy has no weak point," replied the Commander, "make one."

It was he who telegraphed to Joffre during the first battle of the Marne: "The enemy is attacking my flank. My rear is threatened. I am therefore attacking in front."

Foch is a great student, an especial admirer of Napoleon, whose campaigns he had thoroughly studied. Even the campaigns of Cæsar he had found valuable and had gathered from them practical suggestions for his own campaigns. He is the hero of the Marne, the man who on September 9th marched his army between Von Bülow and Von Hausen's Saxons, drove the Prussian Guards into the marshes of St. Gond and forced both Prussians and Saxons into their first great retreat. Later his armies fought on the Yser while the British were battling at Ypres. During the battle of the Somme he was on the English right pressing to Peronne.

For a time he became Chief of the French Staff, until he was called into the field again to his great command. Foch was one of those French officers who had felt that war was sure to come, and had constantly urged that France should be kept in a state of preparedness. The appointment of General Foch to the Supreme Command was largely the result of American urgency.

General March, the American Chief of Staff, in one of his weekly announcements, stated: "One of the most striking things noticeable in the situation as it is shown on the western front is the supreme importance of having a single command. The acceptance of the principle of having a single command, which was advocated by the President of the United States and carried through under his constant pressure, is one of the most important single military things that has been done as far as the Allies are concerned. The unity of command which Germany has had from the

GERMANY'S LAST EFFORT 51

start of the war has been a very important military asset, and we already see the supreme value of having that central command which now has been concentrated in General Foch."

General March, who had earlier been appointed Chief of Staff of the United States army, was sending a steady stream of American troops to Europe, a fact whose importance was well understood by the new Commander-in-Chief. On General March's promotion General Foch sent him the following message:

> I hear with deep satisfaction of your promotion to the rank of General. I associate myself to the just pride which you must feel in evoking the names of your glorious predecessors, Grant and Sheridan. I convey to you my sincere congratulations and I am happy to see you assume permanently the huge task of Chief of Staff of the United States army which you are already performing in so brilliant a way.

General March replied:

> Your message of congratulation upon my promotion to the grade of General Chief of Staff, United States army, was personally conveyed to me by General Vignal, French Military Attaché. I appreciate deeply your most kindly greetings and in expressing my most sincere thanks, avail myself of the opportunity to assure you of

every assistance and constant support which may lie in my power to aid you in the furtherance and successful accomplishment of your great task.

General Foch took command at a very critical time. The Germans had prepared the most formidable drive in the history of the war. They had gathered immense masses of munitions and supplies. Their great armies had been refitted and they were in hopes of a victory which would end the war. Their great offensive had many phases. It resulted in the development of three great salients, the first in Picardy and in the direction of Amiens along the Somme, which was launched on March 21st; the second on the Lys, which was launched on April 9th; and the third which is called the Oise-Marne salient, launched on May 27th.

Between the attacks which developed these salients there were also some unsuccessful attacks of almost equal power. On March 28th there was a desperate struggle to capture Arras, preceded by a bombardment as great as any during the whole offensive, but this at-

GERMANY'S LAST EFFORT 53

tack was defeated with enormous losses to the German troops. A fourth phase of the German offensive took place on June 9th, on a front of twenty miles between Noyon and

THE LAST DESPERATE DRIVES OF THE GERMANS

Montdidier, which gained a few miles at an enormous cost.

On July 15th came the last of the great offensives. It was a smash on a sixty-mile line from Château-Thierry up the Marne, around Rheims, and then east to a few miles west of the Argonne forest. This offensive at the start made a penetration of from three to five miles, but was held firmly and much of the gain lost, through the counter attacks of the Allies. It was at this point that the American troops first began to be seriously felt, and it was at this point that General Foch took up the story, and began the great series of Allied drives which were to crush the German power. But there had been many days of great anxiety before the turn of the tide.

The objects of the German drives were doubtless more or less dependent upon their success. The first drive in Picardy, in the direction of Amiens, had apparently as its object to drive a wedge between the French and British and the object was so nearly attained that only the heroic work of General Carey saved the Allies from disaster.

The Fifth British army, which had borne the brunt of the German attack, had found itself almost crushed by the sheer weight of

GERMANY'S LAST EFFORT 55

numbers. The whole line was broken up and it seemed as if the road was open to Amiens. French reinforcements could not come up in time; bridges could not be blown up because the engineers were all killed. Orders came to General Carey at two o'clock in the morning, March 26th, to hold the gap. He at once proceeded to gather an extemporized army.

Every available man was rounded up, among others a body of American engineers. Laborers, sappers, raw recruits as well as soldiers of every arm. There were plenty of machine guns, but few men knew how to handle them. With this scratch army in temporary trenches, he lay for six days, and as Lloyd George said, "They held the German army and closed that gap on the way to Amiens."

During this fight General Carey rode along the lines shouting encouraging words to his hard-pressed men. He did not know whether he would get supplies of ammunition and provisions or not, but he stuck to it. Later on the regular troops arrived. The American engineers, who had been fighting, immediately returned to their base, and resumed work laying out trenches. General Rawlinson, Commander of the British army at that point, sent the commanding officer of the Americans engaged, the following letter:

> The army Commander wishes to record officially his appreciation of the excellent work your regiment has done in assisting the British army to resist the enemy's powerful offensive during the last ten days. I fully realize that it has been largely due to your assistance that the enemy has been checked, and I rely on you to assist us still further during the few days that are still to come before I shall be able to relieve you in the line. I consider your work in the line to be greatly enhanced by the fact that for six weeks previous to your taking your place in the front line your men had been working at such high pressure erecting heavy bridges on the Somme. My best congratulations and warm thanks to all.
>
> RAWLINSON.

The demoralization of General Gough's Fifth army, which had thus left an eight-mile gap on the left, and which had been saved at that point by General Carey, permitted also the opening of another gap between its right wing and the Sixth French army. Here General Fayolle did with organized troops what

GERMANY'S LAST EFFORT 57

Carey had done with his volunteers further north. The reason for the success of both Carey and Fayolle appears to have been that the German armies had been so thoroughly battered that they were unable to take advantage of the situation. Their regiments had been mixed up, their officers had been separated from their men in the rush of the attack, and before they could recover the opportunity was lost.

The first days of April saw the end of the drive toward Amiens. The Germans claimed the capture of ninety thousand prisoners and one thousand three hundred guns. They had penetrated into the Allies' territory in some points a distance of thirty-five miles. Their new line extended southwest from Arras beyond Albert to the west of Moreuil, which is about nine miles south of Amiens, and then went on west of Pierrepont and Montdidier, curving out at Noyon to the region of the Oise.

The first part of April was a comparative calm, when suddenly there developed the second drive of the German offensive. This drive was not so extensive as the first one, and its object appeared to be to break through the British forces in Flanders and reach the Channel ports. It resulted in a salient embracing an area about three hundred and twenty square miles, and the Germans claimed the capture of twenty thousand prisoners and two hundred guns. It was at this point that General Haig issued his famous order in which he described the British armies as standing with their "backs to the wall." It read as follows:

> Three weeks ago today the enemy began his terrific attacks against us on a fifty-mile front. Its objects are to separate us from the French, to take the Channel ports, and to destroy the British army. In spite of throwing already one hundred and six divisions into the battle and enduring the most reckless sacrifice of human life, he has yet made little progress toward his goals. We owe this to the determined fighting and self-sacrifice of our troops. Words fail me to express the admiration which I feel for the splendid resistance offered by all ranks of our army under the most trying circumstances. Many among us now are tired. To those I would say that victory will belong to the side which holds out the longest. The French army is moving rapidly and in great force to our support. There is no other course open to us but to fight it out. Every position must be

GERMANY'S LAST EFFORT 59

held to the last man. There must be no retiring. With our backs to the wall and believing in the justice of our cause each one of us must fight to the end. The safety of our homes, and the freedom of mankind depend alike upon the conduct of each one of us at this critical moment.

The British Commander's order made the situation clear to the British people and to the world. The Germans had given up for the moment their attempt to divide the British and French armies, and were now attempting to seize the Channel ports, and the British were fighting with true British pluck with their "backs to the wall."

One can imagine the anxiety in the villages of Flanders where they watched the German advance and heard the terrible bombardment which was destroying their beautiful little cities, and threatening to put them under the dominion of the brutal conquerors of Belgium. Town after town fell to the enemy until at last the German attack began to weaken.

Counter attacks on April 17th recaptured the villages of Wytschaete and Meteren. At other points German attacks were repulsed, and the attack on the Lys had reached its limits. It had not only failed to reach the coast but it had not even reached so far as to force the evacuation of Ypres or to endanger Arras. On the contrary the Germans had paid for their advance by such terrible losses that the ground that they had gained meant almost nothing. They then made, on April 30th, a vigorous endeavor to broaden the Amiens salient in the region of Hangard and Noyon. This attack also failed.

On May 27th Ludendorff made his next move. This was in the south, and was preceded by the most elaborate preparations over a forty-mile front. At first it met with great success. German troops from a point northwest of Rheims to Montdidier were moving apparently with the purpose of breaking the French lines and clearing the way for a drive to Paris. Consternation reigned among Allied observers as the Germans carried, apparently with ease, first the formidable Chemin des Dames, which was believed invulnerable, and then the south bank of the Aisne, with its great fortifications at Soissons.

Criticism began to appear of General Foch, who was thought at first to have been taken by surprise. The Germans were using four hundred thousand of their best troops, and the greatest force of tanks, machine guns and poison-gas projectors which they had ever gathered. They captured over forty-five thousand prisoners and took four hundred guns. They penetrated thirty miles and gained six hundred and fifty square miles of territory, but they were held on the River Marne.

It is now apparent that General Foch knew exactly what he was about. He might easily by sending in reinforcements, have put up the same desperate resistance to the German offensive which they were now meeting in other sectors. But he preferred to retreat and lead the enemy on to a position which would make them vulnerable to the great counter attack he was preparing for them on their flank. The Germans reached the Marne, but they paid for it in the terrible losses which they incurred.

The German line now from Montdidier, the extreme point of the Amiens salient, to Château-Thierry, the point of the new Marne salient, was in the form of a bow, and on June 9th General Ludendorff attempted to straighten out the line. His new attack was made on a twenty-mile front between Montdidier and Noyon in the direction of Compiègne. This was another terrific drive and at first gained about seven miles. French counter attacks, however, not only held him in a vise but regained a distance of about one mile. This battle was probably the most disastrous one fought by the Germans during their whole offensive. Nearly four hundred thousand men were completely used up, without gaining the slightest strategic success.

Then followed a period without battles of major importance, during which General Foch by periodic assaults on the Lys, the Somme, on the flanks of Montdidier and Soissons, on the Château-Thierry sector and southwest of

GERMANY'S LAST EFFORT

Rheims, captured many important positions and kept the enemy in constant anxiety.

During the great German offensives the Germans had lost at least five hundred thousand men, while the casualties of the Allies were barely one hundred and fifty thousand. The Germans also were beginning to lose their morale. They were finding that however great might be their efforts, however terrible might be their losses, they were still being constantly held. Their troops were now apparently made of inferior material, and included boys, old men and even convicts.

The system of making attacks by means of shock troops was producing the inevitable result. The shock regiments were composed of selected men, picked here and there, from the regular troops. Their selection had naturally weakened the regiments from which they were taken. After three months of great offensives these shock troops were now in great part destroyed, and the German lines were being held mainly by the inferior troops which had been left. Moreover, in other parts of the world, the allies of Germany were being beaten. In Italy and Albania and Macedonia there was danger.

The Germans prepared for one more effort. On June 18th they had made a costly attempt to carry Rheims. On July 15th they made their last drive. Ludendorff took almost a month for preparation. He gathered together seventy divisions and great masses of munitions, and then drove in from Château-Thierry on a sixty-mile line up on the Marne, and then east to the Argonne forests. His line made a sort of semicircle around Rheims and then pushed south to the east and west of that fortress.

Once again he had temporary success. West of Rheims he penetrated a distance of five miles, and on the first day, had crossed the Marne at Dormans, but was held sharply by Americans east of Château-Thierry. On the second day he made further gains, but with appalling losses. On the 17th he was still struggling on with minor successes but on July 18th the French and Americans launched

GERMANY'S LAST EFFORT

the great counter-offensive from Château-Thierry along a twenty-five mile front, between the Marne and the Aisne. The Germans everywhere began their retreat and the war tide had turned.

The German attack east of Rheims had been a failure from the start. The Allied forces retired about two miles and then held firm. The country there is flat and sandy and gave little shelter to the attacking forces which lost terribly. In this sector, too, there were many American troops, who behaved with distinguished bravery.

By this time nearly seven hundred thousand men of the American army were on the battle line. They had been fighting here and there among the French and English but on June 22d General March announced that five divisions of these troops had been transferred to the direct command of General Pershing as a nucleus for an American army.

In glancing back at the great German drives which have now been described, one is impressed by the terrific character of the fighting. This struggle undoubtedly was the greatest exertion of military power in the history of the world. Never before had such masses of munitions been used; never before had scientific knowledge been so drawn on in the service of war. Thousands of airplanes were patrolling the air, sometimes scouting, sometimes dropping bombs on hostile troops or on hostile stores, sometimes flying low, firing their machine guns into the faces of marching troops. Thousands upon thousands of great guns were sending enormous projectiles, which made great pits wherever they fell. Swarms of machine guns were pouring their bullets like water from a hose upon the charging soldiers.

One of the most noticeable artillery developments was the long-range gun which off and on during this period was bombarding Paris. This bombardment began on March 23d, when the nearest German line was more than sixty-two miles away. For a time the story was regarded as pure fiction, but it was soon established that the great nine-inch shells which

GERMANY'S LAST EFFORT 67

were dropping into the city every twenty minutes came from the forests of St. Gobain, seven miles back of the French trenches near Laon, and about seventy-five miles from Paris. This was another of those futile bits of frightfulness in which the Germans reveled. Military advantage gained by such a gun was almost nothing, and the expense of every shot was out of all proportion to the damage inflicted. It only roused intense indignation and stirred the Allies to greater determination. The first day's casualties in Paris were ten killed and fifteen wounded. By the next day one would not have been able to tell from the Paris streets that such a bombardment was going on at all. The subway and surface cars were running, the streets were thronged and traffic was going on as usual. About two dozen shells were thrown into Paris every day, mainly in the Montmartre district, in a radius of about a mile. This seemed to show that the gun was immovable.

On March 29th, however, a shell struck the church of St. Gervais during the Good Friday service, killing seventy-five persons, and wounding ninety. Fifty-four of those killed were women. The church had been struck at the moment of the Elevation of the Host. This outrage aroused special indignation, and Pope Benedict sent a protest to Berlin.

An examination of exploded shells indicated that the new German gun was less than nine inches in caliber, and that the projectiles, which weighed about two hundred pounds, contained two charges, in two chambers connected by a fuse which often exploded more than a minute apart. It took three minutes for each shell to travel to Paris and it was estimated that such a shell rose to a height of twenty miles from the earth. Three of these guns were used. One of these guns exploded on March 29th, killing a German lieutenant and nine men. The Kaiser was present when the gun was first used. It was said by American scientists that seismographs in the United States felt the shock of each discharge. On April 9th French aviators discovered the location of the new guns, and French artillery began to drop enormous shells weighing half a ton each near the German monsters. A few days later a French shell fell on the barrel of one of these guns and put it out of commission. Great craters were made around the other, interfering with its use, and toward the end of the period it was only occasionally that the remaining gun was fired, and no great damage resulted.

Another feature of the great German drives was the tremendous destruction that accompanied them. Not only were churches, public buildings, and private houses throughout almost the whole district turned into ruin, but the very ground itself was plowed up into craters and shell holes, and the trees smashed into mere splinters. During the whole campaign poison gas of various kinds was used in immense quantities, and it was constantly necessary for the troops to wear gas masks. Sometimes after a town had been evacuated by the enemy it was so filled with gas that it was impossible for victorious troops to enter. One of the fiercest bombardments was that directed against the Portuguese during the fighting along the Lys. The enemy made a special attempt to crush the

Portuguese contingent which behaved with the utmost gallantry, in some cases fighting until their last man had been killed.

It was the season of the year when the orchards were covered with blossoms and the fields with flowers, but the horrors of war destroyed the beauty of the Spring. In these battles men fought until they were completely exhausted and one could see troops staggering as they walked and leaning on each other from pure exhaustion.

These were days when wonders were performed by the Medical Departments of the Allied armies, and the work of the Red Cross was almost as important as the work of the soldiers. Relief for the wounded had to be undertaken and carried on on a mammoth scale. Many of the doctors, nurses, orderlies and ambulance men lost their lives while making efforts to rescue the wounded.

These were days when the German leaders were filled with the pride of victory. They were talking now about a hard German peace.

Photo by Press Illustrating Service.

THE GERMAN GENERAL STAFF

von Mackensen   von Moltke   **Cr. Pr.** Wilhelm   von François   von Falkenhayn   **von Beseler**   von Bethmann-Hollweg
von Bülow   Duke Albrecht   Ludendorf   von Kluck   von Einem   **von Hindenburg**   von Heeringen
Crown Prince Rupprecht   Kaiser Wilhelm II   von Haeseler   von Tirpitz
von Emmich

GERMANY'S LAST EFFORT 71

On June 17th the German Kaiser celebrated the thirtieth anniversary of his accession to the throne. He talked no more of a war of self-defense, but declared the war to be the struggle of two world views wrestling with each other. "Either German principles of right, freedom, honor and morality must be upheld, or Anglo-Saxon principles with their idolatry of Mammon must be victorious." He sent congratulations to Field Marshal Von Hindenburg, to General Ludendorff and to the Crown Prince. Von Hindenburg assured the Kaiser of the unswerving loyalty until death of Germany's sons at the front, and concluded "May our old motto 'Forward with God for King and Fatherland, for Kaiser and Empire' result in many years of peace being granted to your Majesty after our victorious return home."

But the terrific attacks which the German Commanders directed upon the Americans at Château-Thierry and at other points upon the southern lines show well that they knew that there was another danger rising to confront them; that during their great drives a million and a half American soldiers had been learning the art of war, and that every moment of delay meant a new danger. By the end of this period the Americans had arrived.

CHAPTER V

CHATEAU-THIERRY, FIELD OF GLORY

NOWHERE in American history may be found a more glorious record than that which crowned with laurel the American arms at Château-Thierry. Here the American Marines and divisions comprising both volunteers and selected soldiers, were thrown before the German tide of invasion like a huge khaki-colored breakwater. Germany knew that a test of its empire had come. To break the wall of American might it threw into the van of the attack the Prussian Guard backed by the most formidable troops of the German and Austrian empires. The object was to put the fear of the Hun into the hearts of the Yankees, to overwhelm them, to drive straight through them as the prow of a battleship shears through a heavy sea. If America could be defeated, Germany's way to a speedy victory was at hand. If America held—well, that way lay disaster.

And the Americans held. Not only did they hold out but they counter-attacked with such bloody consequences to the German army that Marshal Foch, seizing the psychological moment for his carefully prepared counter-offensive, gave the word for a general attack.

With Château-Thierry and the Marne as a hinge, the clamp of the Allies closed upon the defeated Germans. From Switzerland to the North Sea the drive went forward, operating as huge pincers cutting like chilled steel through the Hindenburg and the Kriemhild lines. It was the beginning of autocracy's end, the end of *Der Tag* of which Germany had dreamed.

The matchless Marines and the other American troops suffered a loss that staggered America. It was a loss, however, that was well worth while. The heroic young Americans who held the might of Germany helpless and finally rolled them back defeated from the field of battle, and who paid for that victory with

Photo by International Film Service. **AMERICA GETS INTO THE WAR AT CANTIGNY**

On the morning of May 28, 1918, the 1st Division, A. E. F., launched its first attack, which took place at Cantigny. Within 45 minutes all objectives had been gained, serious losses inflicted on the enemy, and 200 prisoners taken. General Pershing personally directed operations. This picture shows American troops going forward under support of tanks.

CHATEAU-THIERRY 75

their lives, made certain the speedy end of the world's bloodiest war.

The story of the American army's effective operations in France from Cantigny to the reduction of the St. Mihiel salient, is one long record of victories. To the glory of American arms must be recorded the fact that at no time and at no place in the World War did the American forces retreat before the German hosts.

In the latter days of May, 1918, the Allied forces in France seemed near defeat. The Germans were steadily driving toward Paris. They had swept over the Chemin des Dames and the papers from day to day were chronicling wonderful successes. The Chemin des Dames had been regarded as impregnable, but the Germans passed it apparently without the slightest difficulty. They were advancing on a forty-mile front and on May 28th had reached the Aisne, with the French and British steadily falling back. The anxiety of the Allies throughout the world was indescribable. This was the great German "Victory Drive" and each day registered a new Allied defeat. Newspaper headlines were almost despairing.

On May 29th, however, in quiet type, under great headlines announcing a German gain of ten miles in which the Germans had taken twenty-five thousand prisoners and crossed two rivers, had captured Soissons, and were threatening Rheims, there appeared in American papers a quiet little despatch from General Pershing. It read as follows:

"This morning in Picardy our troops attacked on a front of one and one-fourth miles, advanced our lines, and captured the village of Cantigny. We took two hundred prisoners, and inflicted on the enemy severe losses in killed and wounded. Our casualties were relatively small. Hostile counter-attacks broke down under our fire." This was the first American offensive.

The American troops had now been in Europe almost a year. At first but a small force, they had been greeted in Paris and in London with tremendous enthusiasm. Up to this point they had done little or nothing, but the

CHATEAU-THIERRY 77

small force which passed through Paris in the summer of 1917 had been growing steadily. By this time the American army numbered more than eight hundred thousand men. They had been getting ready; in camps far behind the lines they had been trained, not only by their own officers, but by some of the greatest experts in the French and the British armies. Thousands of officers and men who, but a few months before, had been busily engaged in civilian pursuits, had now learned something of the art of war. They had been supplied with a splendid equipment, with great guns and with all the modern requirements of an up-to-date army.

For some months, here and there, on the French and British lines, small detachments of American troops flanked on both sides by the Allied forces, had been learning the art of war. Here and there they had been under fire. At Cantigny itself they had resisted attack. On May 27th General Pershing had reported "In Picardy, after violent artillery preparations, hostile infantry detachments succeeded in penetrating our advance positions in two points. Our troops counter-attacked, completely expelling the enemy and entering his lines." They had also been fighting that day in the Woevre sector where a raiding party had been repulsed. There had been other skirmishes, too, in which many Americans had won honors both from Great Britain and France. But the attack at Cantigny was the first distinct American advance.

The Americans penetrated the German positions to the depth of nearly a mile. Their artillery completely smothered the Germans, and its whirr could be heard for many miles in the rear. Twelve French tanks supported the American infantry. The artillery preparation lasted for one hour, and then the lines of Americans went over the top. A strong unit of flame throwers and engineers aided the Americans. The American barrage moved forward a hundred yards in two minutes and then a hundred yards in four minutes. The infantry followed with clock-like precision. Fierce hand-to-hand fighting occurred in

CHATEAU-THIERRY 79

Cantigny, which contained a large tunnel and a number of caves. The Americans hurled hand grenades like baseballs into these shelters.

The attack had been carefully planned and was rehearsed by the infantry with the tanks. In every detail it was under the direction of the Superior French Command, to whom much of the credit for its success was due. The news of the American success created general satisfaction among the French and English troops. The operation, of course, was not one of the very greatest importance. It was a sort of an experiment, but coming as it did, in the middle of the great German Drive, it was ominous. America had arrived.

On May 30th General Pershing announced the complete repulse of further enemy attacks from the new American positions near Cantigny. This time he says: "There was considerable shelling with gas, but the results obtained were very small. The attempt was a complete failure. Our casualties were very light. We have consolidated our positions."

The London *Evening News* commenting on this fact says: "Bravo the young Americans! Nothing in today's battle narrative from the front is more exhilarating than the account of their fight at Cantigny. It was clean cut from beginning to end, like one of their countrymen's short stories, and the short story of Cantigny is going to expand into a full-length novel which will write the doom of the Kaiser and Kaiserism. Cantigny will one day be repeated a thousand fold."

The Germans, in reporting this fight, avoided mention of the fact that the operation had been conducted by American troops. This seemed to indicate that they feared the moral effect of such an admission in Germany. Up to this time, with the exception of small brigades, the American army had been held as a reserve. After the Cantigny fight they were hurried to the front. The main point to which they were sent at first was Château-Thierry, north of the Marne, the nearest point to Paris reached by the enemy. There, at the very critical point of the great German Drive, they

CHATEAU-THIERRY

not only checked the enemy but, by a dashing attack, threw him back.

This may be said to be the turning point in the whole war. It not only stopped the German Drive at this point, but it gave new courage to the Allies and took the heart out of the Germans. The troops were rushed to the battle front at Thierry, arriving on Saturday, June 1st. They entered the battle enthusiastically, almost immediately after they had arrived. A despatch from Picardy says: "On their way to the battle lines they were cheered by the crowds in the villages through which they passed; their victorious stand with their gallant French Allies, so soon after entering the line, has electrified all France."

General Pershing's terse account of what happened reads as follows: "In the fighting northwest of Château-Thierry our troops broke up an attempt of the enemy to advance to the south through Veuilly Woods, and by a counter-attack drove him back to the north of the woods."

The American troops had gone into the action only an hour or so after their arrival on the banks of the River Marne. Scarcely had they alighted from their motor trucks when they were ordered into Château-Thierry with a battalion of French-Colonial troops. The

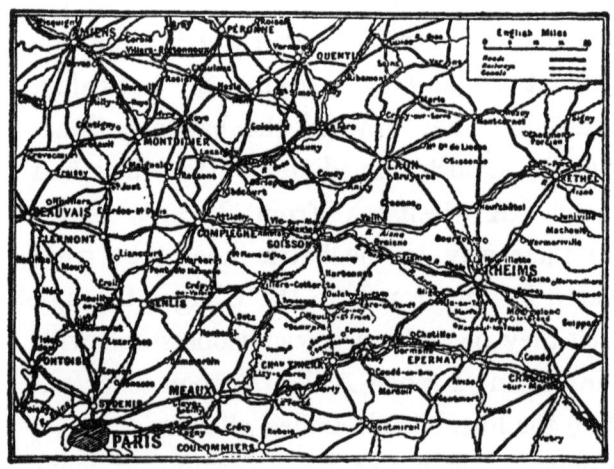

WHERE THE "YANKS" FOUGHT THE SECOND BATTLE OF THE MARNE

enemy were launching a savage drive, and at first succeeded in driving the Americans out of the woods of Veuilly-la-Poterie. But the Americans at once counter-attacked, driving their opponents from their position, and regaining possession of the woods. On the same

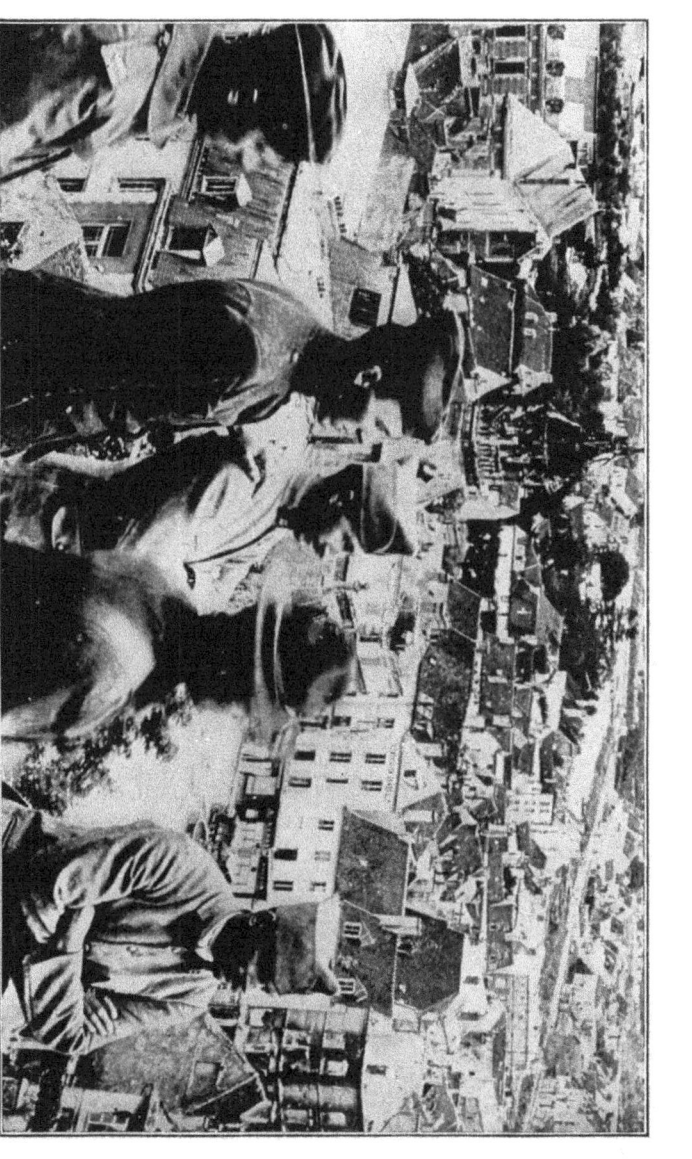

© Committee on Public Information. From Underwood and Underwood, N. Y.

CHÂTEAU-THIERRY, WHERE AMERICA INFLICTED A SECOND GETTYSBURG ON GERMANY

Poilus and Yanks in the foreground looking over the roofs of Château-Thierry, where, in the middle of July in the last year of the war the Americans at a crucial moment stopped the German advance in the second battle of the Marne. After that Germany never

CHATEAU-THIERRY

day the Germans launched an attack of shock troops, attempting to gain a passage across the Marne at Jaulgonne. They obtained a footing on the southern bank but another American counter attack forced them back across the river. The American soldiers were fighting with wonderful spirit, and the French papers were filled with praise of their work. As they came up to go into the line they were singing, and they charged, cheering.

On June 6th came a climax of the American fighting. It was the attack of the American Marines in the direction of Torcy. This gained more than two miles over a two and a half mile front. On the next day the advance continued over a front of nearly six miles, and during the night the Americans captured Bouresches and entered Torcy.

The fighting at Torcy was characteristically American; the Marines advanced yelling like Indians, using bayonet and rifle. From Torcy the Marines set forward and took strong ground on either side of Belleau Wood. They had reached all the objectives and pushed beyond them. The Germans were on the run, and surrendering right and left to the Americans. The attack by the Marines forestalled an attack by the enemy. German reports now noticed the Americans. Their report on June 9th referring to this attack, says: "Americans who attempted to attack northwest of Château-Thierry were driven back beyond their positions of departure with heavy losses and prisoners were captured." The Americans had lost heavily, and the hospitals were filled with their wounded, but the thorough American organization was giving the wounded every care, and the Americans were still moving forward.

On June the 10th, another attack was made on the German lines in the Belleau Wood, which penetrated for about two-thirds of a mile, leaving the Germans in possession of only the northern fringe of the Wood. On June 11th the official statement of the French War Office declared: "South of the Ourcq River the American troops this morning bril-

CHATEAU-THIERRY 85

liantly captured Belleau Wood, and took three hundred prisoners."

Belleau Wood had been considered an almost impregnable position, but the valiant fighting of the American Marines had carried them past it. Fighting here was not merely a series of exciting engagements, but an important action, which may have turned, and very probably did turn, the whole tide of battle. The Americans put three German divisions out of business, and caused a change in the German plans, by preventing an extending movement to Meaux, which was the German objective.

From this time on the confidence shown in all reports from the Allies in France was strengthened. They had found that the Americans were all that they had hoped for, and they were sure now that they could hold on until the full American strength could be brought to bear. General Pershing himself was full of optimism and his fine example stimulated his troops. From this time on all dispatches show that the Americans were more and more getting in the game. Repeated German attacks against their forces, on the Belleau-Bouresches line were repulsed, in spite of the fact that crack German divisions, who had been picked especially to punish them, had been found on their front. It was later found that these divisions had been suddenly ordered to that point "in order to prevent at all costs the Americans being able to achieve success." The German High Command was apparently anxious to prevent American success from stimulating the morale of the Allied army.

During the rest of the summer the Americans took an active part in Foch's great offensive which ultimately crushed the German army. They were heard from at widely divergent points: in Alsace, about Château-Thierry, at Montdidier, and in the British lines.

Most of the fighting during June indicated a slow advance at Château-Thierry. On June 19th the Americans crossed the Marne, near that city. But Château-Thierry itself was not

French Official Photograph by International Film Service.

WIPING OUT THE ST. MIHIEL SALIENT

The first major exploit carried out independently by the American army was the obliteration of the St. Mihiel salient, which had been in German hands since 1914, a spectacular achievement, carried out in two days with great brilliance and precision. The picture shows U. S. troops following the Germans through Thiaucourt, one of the towns on the salient.

CHATEAU-THIERRY 87

captured until the middle of July. On June 29th they participated in a raid near Montdidier and on July 2nd captured Vaux. In the week of July 4th news came of American success in the Vosges. On July 18th they advanced close to Soissons. On August 3rd the Americans captured Fismes, and then for nearly a month made little actual progress, though bitter fighting went on in the country around Fismes and near Soissons. On August 29th after a furious battle they captured the plain of Juvigny, north of Soissons.

In all these battles the Americans were doing their part at difficult points, during the great French drive which was clearing out the Marne salient.

On the 12th of September, the first American army, assisted by certain French units, and under the direct command of General Pershing, launched an attack against the St. Mihiel salient. This was the most important operation of the American troops in the Great War. It was a complete success. September 12th was the fourth anniversary of the establishment of the salient, which reached out from the German line in the direction of Verdun.

The attack was fighting on a grand scale, and that such an operation should be intrusted to the American army indicated an entirely new phase of America's participation in the war. It was preceded by a barrage lasting four hours. The German troops, though probably suspecting that such an attack was coming, were nevertheless surprised. The American attack was on the southern leg of the salient along a distance of twelve miles. The French attacked on the western side from a front of eight miles. Each attack was eminently successful. On the southern front the Americans reached their first objectives at some points an hour ahead of schedule time. Thiaucourt was captured early in the drive; later the Americans gained possession of Nonsard, Pannes, and Bouillonville.

At first the resistance of the Germans, without being tame, was not actually stiff, and the doughboys were able to sweep toward the second line of any position without difficulty.

ST. MIHIEL SALIENT, SHORTLY AFTER THE AMERICAN ATTACK BEGAN

There, however, the Germans began to defend themselves sharply, which delayed, but did not stop the American advance. The attack was made in two waves and carried the American forces a distance of about five miles.

The next day the attack continued, and General Pershing's dispatch stated: "In the St. Mihiel sector we have achieved further successes. The junction of our troops advancing from the south of the sector with those advancing from the west has given us possession of the whole salient to points twelve miles northeast of St. Mihiel, and has resulted in the capture of many prisoners. Forced back by our steady advance the enemy is retiring, and is destroying large quantities of material as he goes. The number of prisoners counted has risen to 13,300. Our line now includes Herbeville, Thillet, Hattonville, St. Benoit, Xammes, Jaulny, Thiaucourt and Vieville."

The salient was wiped out, and the St. Mihiel front reduced from forty to twenty miles.

The first American regiment stationed in the St. Mihiel sector was the 370th Infantry, formerly the Eighth Illinois, a Negro regiment officered entirely by soldiers of that race. This regiment was one of the three that occupied a sector at Verdun when a penetration there by the Germans would have been disastrous to the Allied cause.

The St. Mihiel salient had no great military value to the Germans, and was probably held by them from a sentimental motive. It represented the desperate efforts made by the Crown Prince in his early drive against Verdun. Its destruction, however, was of great importance to the French. It was not only a removal of a menace to the French citizens of Verdun, but it released the French armies at that point for active offensive operation. It also liberated the railway line from Verdun to Nancy, which was of the utmost value to General Pershing and the French armies to his left. It also later developed that the French command regarded the reduction of the St. Mihiel salient as the corner stone of a great encircling movement aimed at the German fortress of Metz. The moral effect of its reduction was also notable as it was one more sign of the weakening of the Germans.

History usually concerns itself with the deeds of humanity in the mass and with the leaders of these masses. It is eminently fitting, however, that this history should record the impressions made upon the mind of an American soldier by a modern battle. The United States Government singled out of all the letters received from the front, that written by Major Robert L. Denig, of Philadelphia, to his wife. The letter is now part of the archives of the War Department, and occupies the highest place of literary honor in the records of the Marines. It describes the operation against the Germans on the Marne on July 18th, 1918. This was the counter-attack led by the Marines which broke the back of the German invasion. Major Denig wrote:

> The day before we left for this big push we had a most interesting fight between a fleet of German planes and a French observation balloon, right over our heads. We saw five planes circle over our town, then put on, what we thought afterwards, a sham fight. One of them, after many fancy stunts, headed right for the bal-

CHATEAU-THIERRY 93

loon. They were all painted with our colors except one. This one went near the balloon. One kept right on. The other four shot the balloon up with incendiary bullets. The observers jumped into their parachutes just as the outfit went up in a mass of flame.

The next day we took our positions at various places to wait for camions that were to take us somewhere in France, when or for what purpose we did not know. Wass passed me at the head of his company—we made a date for a party on our next leave. He was looking fine and was as happy as could be. Then Hunt, Keyser and a heap of others went by. I have the battalion and Holcomb the regiment. Our turn to en-buss did not come until near midnight.

We at last got under way after a few big "sea bags" had hit nearby. Wilmer and I led in a touring car. We went at a good clip and nearly got ditched in a couple of new shell holes. Shells were falling fast by now, and as the tenth truck went under the bridge a big one landed near with a crash, and wounded the two drivers, killed two marines and wounded five more. We did not know at the time, and did not notice anything wrong until we came to a crossroad when we found we had only eleven cars all told. We found the rest of the convoy after a hunt, but even then were not told of the loss, and did not find it out until the next day.

We were finally, after twelve hours' ride, dumped in a big field and after a few hours' rest started our march. It was hot as Hades and we had had nothing to eat since the day before. We at last entered a forest; troops seemed to converge on it from all points. We marched some six miles in the forest, a finer one I have never seen—deer would scamper ahead and we could have eaten one raw. At 10 that night without food, we lay down in a pouring rain to sleep. Troops of all kinds passed us in the night—a shadowy stream, over a half-million men. Some French officers told us that they had never seen such concentration since Verdun, if then.

The next day, the 18th of July, we marched ahead through a jam of troops, trucks, etc., and came at last to a ration dump where we fell to and ate our heads off for the first time in nearly two days. When we left there, the men had bread stuck on their bayonets. I lugged a ham. All were loaded down.

Here I passed one of Wass' lieutenants with his hand wounded. He was pleased as Punch and told us the drive was on, the first we knew of it. I then passed a few men of Hunt's company, bringing prisoners to the rear. They had a colonel and his staff. They were well dressed, cleaned and polished, but mighty glum looking.

We finally stopped at the far end of the forest near a dressing station, where Holcomb again took command. This station had been a big fine stone farm but was now a complete ruin—wounded and dead lay all about. Joe Murray came by with his head all done up—his helmet had saved him. The lines had gone on ahead so we were quite safe. Had a fine aero battle right over us. The stunts that those planes did cannot be described by me.

Late in the afternoon we advanced again. Our route lay over an open field covered with dead.

We lay down on a hillside for the night near some captured German guns, and until dark I watched the

CHATEAU-THIERRY 95

cavalry—some four thousand, come up and take positions.

At 3.30 the next morning Sitz woke me up and said we were to attack. The regiment was soon under way and we picked our way under cover of a gas infested valley to a town where we got our final instructions and left our packs. I wished Sumner good luck and parted.

We formed up in a sunken road on two sides of a valley that was perpendicular to the enemy's front; Hughes right, Holcomb left, Sibley support. We now began to get a few wounded; one man with ashen face came charging to the rear with shell shock. He shook all over, foamed at the mouth, could not speak. I put him under a tent, and he acted as if he had a fit.

I heard Overton call to one of his friends to send a certain pin to his mother if he should get hit.

At 8.30 we jumped off with a line of tanks in the lead. For two "kilos" the four lines of Marines were as straight as a die, and their advance over the open plain in the bright sunlight was a picture I shall never forget. The fire got hotter and hotter, men fell, bullets sung, shells whizzed-banged and the dust of battle got thick. Overton was hit by a big piece of shell and fell. Afterwards I heard he was hit in the heart, so his death was without pain. He was buried that night and the pin found.

A man near me was cut in two. Others when hit would stand, it seemed, an hour, then fall in a heap. I yelled to Wilmer that each gun in the barrage worked from right to left, then a rabbit ran ahead and I watched him wondering if he would get hit. Good rabbit—it took my mind off the carnage. Looked for Hughes way over to the right; told Wilmer that I had a hundred dollars and be sure to get it. You think all kinds of things.

About sixty Germans jumped out of a trench and tried to surrender, but their machine guns opened up, we fired back, they ran and our left company after them. That made a gap that had to be filled, so Sibley advanced one of his to do the job, then a shell lit in a machine-gun crew of ours and cleaned it out completely.

At 10.30 we dug in—the attack just died out. I found a hole or old trench and when I was flat on my back I got some protection. Holcomb was next me; Wilmer some way off. We then tried to get reports. Two companies we never could get in touch with. Lloyd came in and reported he was holding some trenches near a mill with six men. Cates, with his trousers blown off, said he had sixteen men of various companies; another officer on the right reported he had and could see forty men, all told. That, with the headquarters, was all we could find out about the battalion of nearly 800. Of the twenty company officers who went in, three came out, and one, Cates, was slightly wounded.

From then on to about 8 P. M. life was a chance and mighty uncomfortable. It was hot as a furnace, no water, and they had our range to a "T." Three men lying in a shallow trench near me were blown to bits.

I went to the left of the line and found eight wounded men in a shell hole. I went back to Cates' hole and three shells landed near them. We thought they were killed, but they were not hit. You could hear men calling for help in the wheat fields. Their cries would get weaker and weaker and die out. The German planes were thick in the air; they were in groups of from three

CHATEAU-THIERRY

to twenty. They would look us over and then we would get a pounding. One of our planes got shot down; he fell about a thousand feet, like an arrow, and hit in the field back of us. The tank exploded and nothing was left.

We had a machine gun officer with us and at six a runner came up and reported that Sumner was killed. He commanded the machine-gun company with us. He was hit early in the fight by a bullet, I hear; I can get no details. At the start he remarked: "This looks easy—they do not seem to have much art." Hughes' headquarters were all shot up. Turner lost a leg.

Well, we just lay there all through the hot afternoon.

It was great—a shell would land near by and you would bounce in your hole.

As twilight came, we sent out water parties for the relief of the wounded. Then we wondered if we would get relieved. At 9 o'clock we got a message congratulating us and saying the Algerians would take over at midnight. We then began to collect our wounded. Some had been evacuated during the day, but at that, we soon had about twenty on the field near us. A man who had been blinded wanted me to hold his hand. Another, wounded in the back, wanted his head patted, and so it went; one man got up on his hands and knees. I asked him what he wanted. He said, "Look at the full moon," then fell dead. I had him buried, and all the rest I could find.

All the time bullets sung and we prayed that shelling would not start until we had our wounded on top.

The Algerians came up at midnight and we pushed out. They went over at daybreak and got all shot up.

We made the relief under German flares and the light from a burning town.

We went out as we came, through the gulley and town, the latter by now all in ruins. The place was full of gas, so we had to wear our masks. We pushed on to the forest and fell down in our tracks and slept all day. That afternoon a German plane got a balloon and the observer jumped and landed in a high tree. It was some job getting him down. The wind came up and we had to dodge falling trees and branches. As it was, we lost two killed and one wounded from that cause.

That night the Germans shelled us and got three killed and seventeen wounded. We moved a bit further back to the crossroad and after burying a few Germans, some of whom showed signs of having been wounded before, we settled down to a short stay.

It looked like rain, and so Wilmer and I went to an old dressing station to salvage some cover. We collected a lot of bloody shelter halves and ponchos that had been tied to poles to make stretchers, and were about to go, when we stopped to look at a new grave. A rude cross made of two slats from a box had written on it:

"Lester S. Wass, Captain U. S. Marines, July 18, 1918."

The old crowd at St. Nazaire and Bordeaux, Wass and Sumner killed, Baston and Hunt wounded, the latter on the 18th, a clean wound, I hear, through the left shoulder. We then moved further to the rear and camped for the night. Dunlap came to look us over. His car was driven by a sailor who got out to talk to a few of the marines, when one of the latter yelled out, "Hey, fellows! Anyone want to see a real live gob,

CHATEAU-THIERRY 99

right this way." The gob held a regular reception. A carrier pigeon perched on a tree with a message. We decided to shoot him. It was then quite dark, so the shot missed. I then heard the following as I tried to sleep: "Hell; he only turned round;" "Send up a flare;" "Call for a barrage," etc. The next day further to the rear still, a Ford was towed by with its front wheels on a truck.

We are now back in a town for some rest and to lick our wounds.

As I rode down the battalion, where once companies 250 strong used to march, now you see fifty men, with a kid second lieutenant in command; one company commander is not yet twenty-one.

After the last attack I cashed in the gold you gave me and sent it home along with my back pay. I have no idea of being "bumped off" with money on my person, as if you fall into the enemy's hands you are first robbed, then buried perhaps, but the first is sure.

Baston, the lieutenant that went to Quantico with father and myself, and of whom father took some pictures, was wounded in both legs in the Bois de Belleau. It was some time before he was evacuated and gas gangrene set in. He nearly lost his legs, I am told, but is coming out O. K. Hunt was wounded in the last attack, got his wounds fixed up and went back again till he had to be sent out. Coffenburg was hit in the hand, —all near him were killed. Talbot was hit twice, but is about again. That accounts for all the officers in the company that I brought over. In the first fight 103 of the men in that outfit were killed or wounded. The second fight must have about cleaned out the old crowd.

The tanks, as they crushed their way through the wet, gray forest looked to me like beasts of the pre-stone age.

In the afternoon as I lay on my back in a hole that I dug deeper, the dark gray German planes with their sinister black crosses, looked like Death hovering above. They were for many. Sumner, for one. He was always saying, "Denig, let's go ashore!" Then here was Wass, whom I usually took dinner with—dead, too. Sumner, Wass, Baston and Hunt—the old crowd that stuck together; two dead, one may never be any good any more; Hunt, I hope, will be as good as ever.

The officers mentioned in Major Denig's letter, with their addresses and next of kin, are:

Lieutenant Colonel Berton W. Sibley; Harriet E. Sibley, mother; Essex Junction, Vt.

First Lieutenant Clifton B. Cates; Mrs. Willis J. Cates, mother; Tiptonville, Tenn.

First Lieutenant Horace Talbot, no next of kin; Woonsocket, R. I.

Captain Arthur H. Turner; Charles S. Turner, father; 188 West River St., Wilkes-Barre, Pa.

Captain Bailey Metcalf Coffenberg; Mrs. Elizabeth Coffenberg; 30 Jackson St., Staten Island, N. Y.

CHATEAU-THIERRY

Captain Albert Preston Baston; Mrs. Ora Z. Baston, mother; Pleasant Avenue, St. Louis Park, Minn.

Captain Lester Sherwood Wass; L. A. Wass, father; Gloucester, Mass.

Captain Allen M. Sumner; Mrs. Mary M. Sumner, wife; 1824 S Street, N. W., Washington, D. C.

Lieutenant Colonel Thomas Holcomb; Mrs. Thomas Holcomb, wife; 1535 New Hampshire Avenue, Washington, D. C.

Second Lieutenant John Laury Hunt; Etta Newman, sister; Gillet, Texas.

Captain Walter H. Sitz; Emil H. Sitz, father; Davenport, Iowa.

First Lieutenant John W. Overton, son of J. M. Overton, 901 Stahlman Building, Nashville, Tenn.

Major Egbert T. Lloyd; Mrs. E. T. Lloyd, wife; 4900 Cedar Avenue, Philadelphia, Pa.

Major Ralph S. Keyser; Charles E. Keyser, father; Thoroughfare, Va.

Captain Pere Wilmer; Mrs. Alice Emory Wilmer, mother; Centerville, Md.

Lieutenant Colonel John A. Hughes; Mrs. A. J. Hughes, wife, care of Rear Admiral William Parks; Post Office Building, Philadelphia, Pa.

Lieutenant Overton was the famous Yale athlete, the intercollegiate one-mile champion.

CHAPTER VI

ENGLAND AND FRANCE STRIKE IN THE NORTH

UP to July 18, 1918, the Allied armies in France had been steadily on the defensive, but on that date the tide turned. General Foch, who had been yielding territory for several months in the great German drives, now assumed the offensive himself and began the series of great drives which was to crush the German power and drive the enemy in defeat headlong from France.

The first of these great blows was the one which began with the appearance of the Americans at Château-Thierry. The Germans had formed a huge salient whose eastern extremity lay near Rheims, and its western extremity west of Soissons. It was like a great pocket reaching down in the direction of Paris from those two points. Against this salient the

French and Americans had directed a tremendous thrust. The Germans resisted with desperation. It was the turning point of the war, but they were compelled to yield. Town after town was regained by the French and American troops, until, by August 5th, the Crown Prince had been driven from the Marne to the Vesle, and the salient had been completely obliterated.

On August 7th General Foch delivered his second blow. During the fighting on the Marne it had often been wondered by those who were observing the great French general's strategy, why the British seemed to make no move. Occasionally there had been reports of minor assaults, either on the Lys salient, far north, or on the Somme and Montdidier sectors, lying between. It had not been noticed that in these minor assaults the English had been obtaining positions of strategic importance, and that they were steadily getting ready for an English offensive.

But their time had now come, and on August 7th the armies of Sir Douglas Haig began an attack against the armies of Prince Rupprecht on the Lys salient. This was followed, on August 8th, by another still greater Allied advance in Picardy, between Albert and Montdidier.

Both of these attacks met with notable success. On the Lys salient the English penetrated a distance of one thousand yards over a four-mile front, and followed up this advance by persistent attacks which led to the reoccupation, on August 19th, of Merville, and on August 31st, of Mont Kemmel. On this front the Germans had weakened their strength by withdrawing troops to aid other parts of their front, and the British were constantly taking advantage of this weakening.

The Germans had found this salient a failure. It had failed to attain its objective, the flanking of the Lens line south. They therefore were steadily retreating without any intention other than to extricate themselves from positions of no value, in the most economical manner. The quick operations of the British, however, led to the capture of many prisoners and a number of machine guns and trench mortars.

The English offensive in Picardy was a more serious matter, and from some points of view was the greatest offensive in the war. The Allied front had been prepared for offensive operations by minor attacks which had secured for the Allied troops dominating positions. The attack was a surprise attack. The Germans were expecting local attacks but not a movement of this magnitude. The surprise was increased because it was made through a heavy mist which prevented observation. It was preceded by tremendous artillery fire which lasted for four minutes, and which was followed by the charge of infantry and tanks. The German artillery hardly replied at all, and only the resistance of a few rifles and machine guns fired vaguely through the fog met the charging troops.

The attack was on a twenty-five-mile front and on the first day gained seven miles, captured seven thousand men and a hundred guns. On the following day there was an advance of about five miles and seventeen thousand more prisoners were captured.

The Germans were now retiring in great haste, blowing up ammunition dumps and abandoning an enormous quantity of stores of all kinds. The English were using cavalry and airplanes, which were flying low over the field and throwing the German troops into confusion. Over three hundred guns, including many of heavy caliber, were captured. The ground had been plowed up by shells and thousands of bodies of men and horses were found lying where they fell. A feature of the attack was the swift whippet tanks which advanced far ahead of the infantry lines.

In the French official report occurred the following statement:

"The brilliant operation which we, in concert with British troops, executed yesterday has been a surprise for the enemy. As occurred in the offensive of July 18th the soldiers of General Debeney have captured enemy soldiers engaged in the peaceful pursuit of harvesting the fields behind the German lines."

By August 10th the Germans had fallen back to a line running through Chaulnes and Roye. Montdidier had been captured, and eleven German divisions had been smashed. By August 12th the number of prisoners was 40,000, and by the 18th the Allied front was almost in the same line as it was in the summer of 1916, before the battle of the Somme.

The next step was to capture Bapaume and Peronne. The French, on August 19th, captured the Lassigny Massif, and continued to press on their attack. Noyon fell on the 29th, Roye on the 27th, Chaulnes on the 29th. Further north the British had captured Albert, and on the 29th occupied Bapaume. On September 1st they took Peronne with two thousand prisoners.

The advance still continued, and the German weakness was becoming more and more apparent. On September 6th the whole Allied line swept forward, with an average penetration of eight miles. Chauny was captured and the fortress of Ham. On September 17th the British were close to St. Quentin and the

IN THE NORTH 109

French in their own old intrenchments before La Fère. On September 18th a surprise advance over a twenty-two-mile front crossed the Hindenburg line at two points north of St. Quentin, Villeret and from Pontru to Hollom.

The first and third British armies, a little further to the north, were moving toward Cambrai and Douai, threatening not only them, but to get in the rear of Lens. This force proceeded up the Albert-Bapaume highway, and on August 27th captured a considerable portion of the Hindenburg line. On the 30th they reached Bullecourt and on September 2d crossed the Drocourt Quéant line on a six-mile front. This was the famous switch line, meant to supplement the Hindenburg line and its capture meant the complete overthrow of the German intrenched positions at this point.

The Germans retreated hastily to the Canal du Nord, and on September 3d Quéant was captured by an advance on a twenty-mile front, along with ten thousand prisoners. The Allied forces were moving steadily forward. On September 18th the British reached the defenses of Cambrai and were encircling the city of St. Quentin. On October 3d the advance upon Cambrai forced the Germans to evacuate the Lens coal fields, and on October 9th another advance over a thirty-mile front enabled the Allies to occupy Cambrai and St. Quentin. On the 11th they had reached the suburbs of Douai. By this time the whole of the Picardy salient had been wiped out.

The preceding summary of this great movement gives little idea of the tremendous struggle which had gone on during these two critical months, and hardly does more than suggest the tremendous importance of the British operations. The Hindenburg line was like a great fortification, and for more than a year had been regarded as impregnable. At Bullecourt there were two main lines. One hundred and twenty-five yards in front of the first line was a belt of wire twenty-five feet broad, so thick that it could not be seen through. The line itself contained double machine-gun emplacements of ferro-concrete, one hundred and twenty-five yards apart, with lesser emplace-

IN THE NORTH

ments between them. More belts of wire protected the support line. Here a continuous tunnel had been constructed at a depth of over forty feet. Every thirty-five yards there were exits with flights of forty-five steps. The tunnels were roofed and lined and bottomed with heavy timber, and numerous rooms branched off. They were lighted by electricity. Large nine-inch trench mortars stood at the traverses and strong machine-gun positions covered the line from behind.

The Hindenburg line was really only one of a series of twenty lines, each connected with the others by communicating trenches. The main lines were solid concrete, separated by an unending vista of wire entanglements. At points this barrier of barbed wire extended in solid formation for ten miles. This tremendous system of defenses was originally called by the Germans the Siegfried line, and in the spring of 1917 they found it wise, at points where a strong offensive was expected, to fall back to it for protection. It had been their hope that it would prove an impassable barrier to the Allied troops, but now it had been broken, and the moral effect of the British success was even greater than the material.

One of the most noticeable results of the British advance had been the capture of Lens. It had been captured without a fight, because of the British threat upon its rear, but its capture was of tremendous importance. Lens had been the scene of bitter fighting in the latter part of August, 1917, when the Canadians had specially distinguished themselves. This city had been heavily fortified by the Germans who had recognized its importance as being the center of the great Lens coal fields, and they had never given it up. It had sometimes been described as the strongest single position that had ever confronted the Allies on the western front. It had been made a sort of citadel of reinforced concrete. Even the courage and power of the Canadians had only given them possession of some of its suburbs. Between these suburbs and the concrete citadel were the coal pits, with their fathomless depths of ages and the mysteries of kultural strategy. The

IN THE NORTH 113

struggle became a succession of avalanches of gas, burning oil, rifle and machine-gun fire. Both sides lost terrifically, but the Germans had held the town. Now it was given up without a blow and its great coal fields were once more in possession of the French. Before retreating the Germans showed their usual destructive energy and the mines were found flooded as a result of consistent and scientific use of dynamite.

The recapture of Lens was cheering news in Paris. Not the least of the many sufferings of the French during the last two years of the war was that which came from the scarcity of coal. Indeed, more than once during those two winters coal could not be obtained at any price. These periods unfortunately came in the latter part of the winter, and it happened they were unusual periods of intense cold. Thousands of people stayed in bed all day in order to keep warm. The capture of Lens, therefore, had been anxiously desired. Nearly the whole of the French coal supply had come from Lens and the adjacent Bethune coal fields. The Bethune field, although steadily working, had never produced enough coal for even the pressing necessities of the French munition works.

The news that Bapaume had fallen on August 29th brought back, especially to the British, memories not only the previous year and of the great forward movement which, on March 17th, had swept them over Bapaume and Peronne, but also bitter memories of the retreat in the previous March, which had carried them back under the overwhelming German pressure. The capture therefore was balm to their spirits, and an English correspondent, Mr. Philip Gibbs, who had accompanied the British on their previous advance, found officers and men full of laughter and full of memories.

On all sides were the battle-fields of 1916 and 1917; Mametz Wood, Belleville Wood, Usna Hill, Ginchy, Morval, Guillemont. The fields were covered with battle débris, and yet to the English it was sacred ground from the graves of the men who fell there. Those

FAMOUS BRITISH GENERALS
General Smith-Dorrien, British Corps Commander in the famous retreat from Mons; Generals Plumer, Rawlinson and Byng, Commanders on the Western Front; General Birdwood, Commander of the Australian-New Zealand troops at Gallipoli.

IN THE NORTH 115

graves still remained. The British shell fire had not touched them, but as the English advanced there were many bodies of gray-clad men on the roads and fields, and dead horses, and a litter of barbed wire, and deep shelters dug under banks, and shell craters, and helmets, gas masks, and rifles thrown here and there by the enemy as they fled. Now it was the Germans that were fleeing, and fleeing hopelessly, sullen, bitter at their officers, impatient of discipline.

One of the great differences between the attacks of the Allies in their last year of the war and those of preceding years, was the increased use and the improved character of the tanks. The tanks were a development of the war. Before the war, however, the development of the caterpillar tractor had suggested to a few far-sighted people the possibility of evolving from this invention a machine capable of offensive use over rough country in close warfare. Experiments were made in behalf of the English War Office for some time without practical results.

At last after these experiments had resulted in various failures, a type of tractor was finally designed which produced satisfactory results. It was a caterpillar tractor, with an endless self-laid track, over which internal driving wheels could be propelled by the engines. It was not until July, 1916, that the first consignment of these new engines of warfare arrived at the secret maneuver ground.

There were two kinds. One called the male was armed with two Hotchkiss quick-fire guns, as well as with an armament of machine guns. The other type, called the female, was armed only with machine guns. The male tank was designed for dealing with the concrete emplacements for the German machine guns. The other was more suitable for dealing with machine-gun personnel and riflemen. Some time was taken in training men to use these tanks, for the crew of a tank must suffer a great deal of hardship; on account of the noise of the engine every command had to be made by signs, and the motion of the tank being like that of a ship on a heavy sea, was likely to produce seasickness.

The tanks were painted with weird colors for the purpose of concealment, and when they first appeared caused a great deal of wonder and amusement. They were first used in battle on September 15, 1916, in a continuation of the battle of the Somme, and proved a great surprise to the Germans. The Germans directed all available rifle and machine-gun fire upon them without success. A correspondent narrates that: "As the 'Crème de Menthe' moved on its way, the bullets fell from its sides harmlessly. It advanced upon a broken wall, leaned up against it heavily, until it fell with a crash of bricks, and then rose on to the bricks and passed over them and walked straight into the midst of factory ruins." They were an immense success and had come to stay. In the course of time, on account of the growing size and importance of the tanks organization, the British established a special Tank Corps by itself, under a Director General. The troops of other nations soon found it necessary to use the new engine of war, and, throughout the year of 1918, the Allied superiority in tanks had much to do with their success.

One more great Allied victory must be briefly referred to. The capture of Cambrai, which took place on the 9th of October, was the climax of weeks of the hardest fighting of the whole year, and the Germans were driven into a flight which was practically a rout. In the series of fights which resulted in this great success the British engaged and defeated thirty-six German divisions, approximately 432,000 men. The final attack was fought by infantry without artillery support, for it was fought in the streets of the city, where every house was a machine-gun fort.

On the previous day the Canadians had captured the Scheldt Canal, which swings in a close loop around the city. The attack was made in the darkness and rain, and every step in advance was bitterly contested. The Germans received numerous reinforcements and counter-attacked again and again with the most

IN THE NORTH

fanatical courage. The British advance was a massacre, and at four o'clock in the morning the Canadian and English troops, pressing in from the north and south of the city, joined hands in the chief square of Cambrai.

This was a city which in the previous year had resisted all British attacks. Its capture was a glorious victory and it was only accomplished after the Allied forces had stormed down the strongest lines ever made in war.

CHAPTER VII

BELGIUM'S GALLANT EFFORT

FOR more than four years Belgium suffered under the iron heel of the German invaders. One little corner in the far west was occupied by her gallant army, fighting with the utmost courage and a patriotism which has won the admiration of the world under its great King Albert, whose heroic leadership had turned the little commercial nation into a nation of heroes. Conditions of life in the Belgian cities were almost intolerable. The great Belgian Relief Commission, under the direction of Mr. Hoover, had kept the people from starvation, but it could not secure them their rights. They lived in the midst of brutality and injustice.

On Belgian Independence Day at London, Arthur J. Balfour, the British Foreign Minister, made an address in which he commented upon the German treatment of Belgium. In the course of his address he said: "Bitter must be the thought in every Belgian heart of what Belgians in Belgium are now suffering. Let them, however, take courage. Let their spirits rise in a mood of profound cheerfulness, for these dark days are not going to last forever, and when they come to a conclusion, when again peace dawns upon this much tormented and cruelly tried world, when Belgium is again free and prosperous, then Belgians, whether they have spent these unhappy years in exile, or, an even harder fate, have spent them in their own country, they will be able to look back upon this time of cruel and unexampled trial, and they will say to themselves, to their children and to their descendants, that Belgium, though her existence as a political entity is less than a century, has within that period shown an example of courage, constancy and virtue to mankind for which all the world should be grateful."

The English Foreign Minister was perhaps

not prophesying. He knew something of what was coming. The Great Offensive which was to free Belgium and her German oppressor was already under way. The first move, however, was not upon land, but upon the sea. In the autumn of 1914 the little Belgian port of Zeebrugge, with the neighboring port of Ostend, was captured by the Germans. The Germans, who had already seized the ship-building plants at Antwerp, then began to build submarines, and sent them down the canals through Bruges to Zeebrugge and Ostend. From these ports they proceeded to attack the English commerce.

In the spring of 1918 submarine attacks on English shipping was so serious that England was using every possible effort to destroy these piratical craft, and it was determined to make an attempt to block the entrances to the canals at Zeebrugge and Ostend, by sinking old ships in the channels.

The expedition took place during the night of April 22d, under the command of Vice-Admiral Sir Roger Keyes. Six obsolete Brit-

BELGIUM'S EFFORT

ish cruisers took part in the expedition. These were the Brilliant, Iphigenia, Sirius, Intrepid, Thetis and Vindictive. The Vindictive carried storming parties to destroy the stone mole at Zeebrugge; the remaining five cruisers were filled with concrete, and it was intended that they should be sunk in the entrances of the two ports. A large force of monitors and small fast craft accompanied the expedition. An observer thus describes the heroic exploit:

The night was overcast and there was a drifting haze. Down the coast a great searchlight swung its beam to and fro in the small wind and short sea. From the Vindictive's bridge, as she headed in toward the mole, there was scarcely a glimmer of light to be seen shoreward. Ahead as she drove through the water rolled the smoke screen, her cloak of invisibility, wrapped about her by small craft. This was the device of Wing-Commander Brock, without which, acknowledged the Admiral in command, the operation could not have been conducted. A northwest wind moved the volume of it shoreward ahead of the ships. Beyond it was the distant town, its defenders unsuspicious.

It was not until the Vindictive, with bluejackets and marines standing ready for landing, was close upon the mole, that the wind lulled and came away again from the southeast, sweeping back the smoke screen and laying her bare to eyes that looked seaward. There was a moment immediately afterward when it seemed to those on the ships as if the dim harbor exploded into light. A star shell soared aloft, then a score of star shells. Wavering beams of the searchlights swung around and settled into a glare. A wild fire of gun flashes leaped against the sky; strings of luminous green beads shot aloft, hung and sank. The darkness of the night was supplemented by a nightmare daylight of battle-fired guns, and machine guns along the mole. The batteries ashore woke to life.

It was in a gale of shelling that the Vindictive laid her nose against the thirty-foot-high concrete side of the mole, let go her anchor, and signalled to the Daffodil to shove her stern in. The Iris went ahead and endeavored to get alongside likewise.

The fire was intense while the ships plunged and rolled beside the mole in the seas, the Vindictive, with her greater draft, jarring against the foundations of the mole with every lunge. They were swept diagonally by machine-gun fire from both ends of the mole and by the heavy batteries on shore. Captain Carpenter conned the Vindictive from the open bridge until her stern was laid in, when he took up his position in the flame thrower hut on the port side. It is marvelous that any occupant should have survived a minute in this hut, so riddled and shattered was it.

The officer of the Iris, which was in trouble ahead of the Vindictive, described Captain Carpenter as handling her like a picket boat. The Vindictive was fitted along her port side with a high, false deck, from which ran eighteen brows, or gangways, by which the storming and demolition parties were to land. The men gathered in readiness on the main lower decks, while Colonel Elliott, who was to lead the marines, waited on the false deck just abaft the bridge. Captain Hallahan, who commanded the bluejackets, was amidships. The word for the assault had not yet been given when both leaders were killed.

The mere landing on the mole was a perilous business. It involved a passage across the crashing and splintering gangways, a drop over the parapet into the field of fire of the German machine-guns which swept its length, and a further drop of some sixteen feet to the surface of the mole itself. Many were killed and more wounded as they crowded up the gangways, but nothing hindered the orderly and speedy landing by every gangway. The lower deck was a shambles, as the Commander made the round of the ship, yet the wounded and dying raised themselves to cheer as he made his tour.

The Iris had trouble of her own. Her first attempts to make fast to the mole ahead of the Vindictive failed, as her grapnels were not large enough to span the parapet. Two officers, Lieutenant-Commander Bradford, and Lieutenant Hawkins, climbed ashore and sat

STORMING THE MOLE AT ZEEBRUGGE

One of the most brilliant and spectacular feats in naval history was the British blocking of the submarine harbor at Zeebrugge. The picture shows one of the detachments of marines that braved the terrific German defense fire and swarmed up the mole that protects the harbor, planting explosives that made a great breach and let the tides in.

astride the parapet trying to make the grapnels fast, till each was killed, and fell down be-

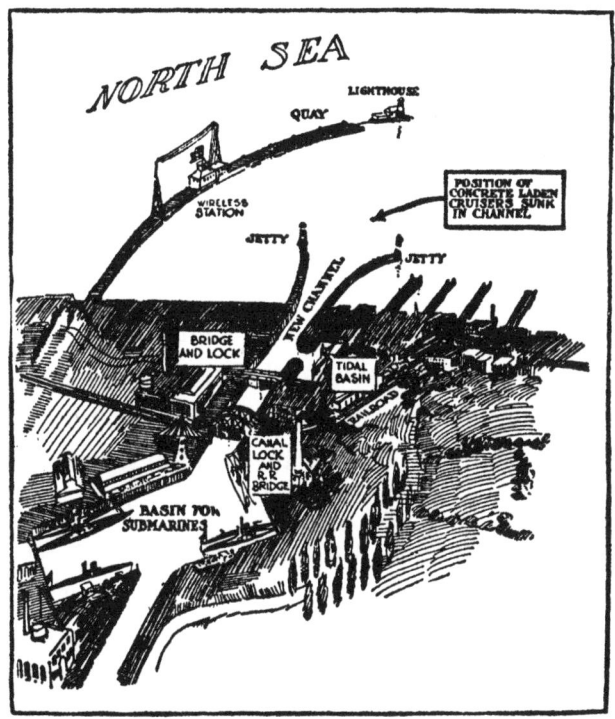

ZEEBRUGGE HARBOR, BLOCKED BY BRITISH

tween the ship and the wall. Commander Valentine Gibbs had both legs shot away, and died next morning. Lieutenant Spencer though wounded, took command and refused to be relieved.

The Iris was obliged at last to change her position and fall in astern of the Vindictive, which suffered very heavily from fire. Her total casualties were eight officers and sixty-nine men killed, and three officers and 103 men wounded.

The storming parties upon the mole met with no resistance from the Germans other than an intense and unremitting fire. One after another buildings burst into flames, or split and crumbled as dynamite went off. A bombing party working up toward the mole in search of the enemy destroyed several machine-gun emplacements but not a single prisoner awarded them. It appears that upon the approach of the ships and with the opening of fire the enemy simply retired and contented themselves with burning machine guns to the short end of the mole.

The object of the fighting on the mole was in large part to divert the enemy's attention while the work of blocking the canals was being accomplished.

Of this operation the official narrative says: "The Thetis came first steaming into a tornado of shells from great batteries ashore. All her crew save a remnant who remained to steam her in and sink her, already had been taken off her by a ubiquitous motor launch. The remnant spared hands enough to keep her four guns going. It was hers to show the road to the Intrepid and Iphigenia which followed. She cleared a string of armed barges, which defends the channel from the tip of the mole, but had the ill-fortune to foul one of her propellers upon a net defense which flanks it on the shore side. The propeller gathered in the net and it rendered her practically unmanageable. Shore batteries found her and pounded her unremittingly. She bumped into the bank, edged off and found herself in the channel again, still some hundreds of yards from the mouth of the canal in practically a sinking condition. As she lay she signalled invaluable directions to others, and her Commander blew charges and sank it. Motor launches took off her crew. The Intrepid, smoking like a volcano, and with all her guns blazing, followed. Her motor launch had failed to get alongside, outside the harbor, and she had men enough for anything. Straight into the canal she steered, her smoke blowing back from her into the Iphigenia's eyes so that the latter was blinded, and going a little wild, ran into the dredger, with her barge moored beside it, which lay at the western arm of the canal. She was not clear though, and entered the canal, pushing the barge before her.

"It was then that a shell hit the steam connections of her whistle and the escape of steam which followed drove off some of the smoke, and let her see what she was doing. Lieutenant Carter, commanding the Intrepid, placed the nose of his ship neatly on the mud of the western bank, ordered his crew away, and blew up his ship by switches in the chart room. Lieutenant Leake, commanding the Iphigenia, beached her according to arrangement on the eastern side, blew her up, saw her drop nicely across the canal, and left her with her engines still going to hold her in position till she should have bedded well down on the bottom. According to the latest reports from air observation the two old ships, with their holds full of concrete, are lying across the canal in a V-position, and it is probable that the work they set out to do has been accomplished and that the canal is effectively blocked."

At Ostend an attempt was also made to block the canal on the same night, but it was unsuccessful owing to a shift of wind which blew away the smoke screen behind which the British craft were acting, and enabled the German gun fire to destroy the flares which had been lit to mark the entrance to the harbor. The cruisers tried to act by guesswork, and one of the block ships was sunk, but it was not in a position to obstruct the canal.

On May 9th another attempt was made, and the Vindictive, filled with concrete, was sunk in the Ostend channel.

This daring exploit of the English fleet,

though it had destroyed the value of Zeebrugge and Ostend as submarine bases, had left the Germans in possession. In September, however, General Foch determined that the time had come to throw his armies against the German forces in the distracted little country. He planned two widely separated thrusts. On the south he sent Pershing against the Germans between the Argonne and the Meuse. They made rapid progress, capturing Montfaucon, Varennes and driving on until they had destroyed the German control of the Paris-Châlons-Verdun Railroad.

This was a serious blow to the Germans, for a further push northward would cut the vital lateral railway connecting the German armies in Belgium and France with those in Alsace-Lorraine. Ludendorff hastened reserves to this front, and the American operation was slowed down. Meanwhile at the other end of the line the Belgians, with General Plumer's Second British Army, suddenly attacked on a front which extended all the way from the canal at Dixmude to the Lys, swept the Germans out of all the famous fighting ground of the Ypres salient, pushed across the Passchendaele Ridge and down into the Flanders plain below.

The situation of the Germans in the Lille regions of the south and also the Belgian coast became at once dangerous. Once more Ludendorff was compelled to send reserves, and this thrust began to slow up but it was not checked permanently, and the Belgian armies were to move on. While this advance was being conducted the British fleet were bombarding the coastal defenses. The Belgian army, fighting with the utmost spirit under command of King Albert, made a penetration of five miles and captured four thousand prisoners and an immense amount of supplies.

On September 30th they captured the city of Roulers. For ten days there was a consolidation of position by the Allies, but on October 14th they made a furious attack in the general direction of Ghent and Courtrai. Thousands of prisoners and several complete batteries of guns were captured. In this attack British,

Belgian and French troops took part, and the troops of the three nations went over the top without preliminary bombardment, taking the enemy by surprise.

On October 15th the news from Flanders showed that the victory was growing in extent, the Allied armies were advancing on a front of about twenty-five miles, and in some places had penetrated the enemy's positions six or seven miles. The Belgians had captured seven thousand prisoners and the British and French about four thousand. In French Flanders the British advanced to a point about three miles west of Lille.

The battle was carried on in a heavy rain which turned the battlefields into seas of mud; while this hampered the Allied troops it hindered even more the Germans in trying to move away their material through the mired ground of the Flanders Lowland.

On the next day dispatches indicated that a retreat on a tremendous scale in northern Belgium was under way. The Germans were retreating so fast that the Allies lost touch with

BELGIUM'S EFFORT 185

the enemy. The gallant little Belgian army, assisted by crack British and French troops, had driven the despoilers of its country from a large section which the Germans had occupied since the early days of the war, and had gained positions of such importance as to make it probable that the Germans would have to abandon the entire coast of Belgium.

Moreover, on the south, the city of Lille, with the great mining and manufacturing districts around it, was being left in a salient which was growing deeper every hour and which the enemy could not hope to hold. At certain points the resistance of the Germans was extraordinarily fierce. This was especially true in the region of Thouret. The battle here was from street to street and from house to house. The Germans had placed machine-guns in the windows of houses and cellars and fired murderous streams of bullets into the advancing Belgians but were unable to stop them.

The Belgians fought with a dogged determination such as only troops fighting to regain their outraged country could display. Nothing could stop them. At other points, especially in the northern part of the battle area, the Germans surrendered freely. Many civilians were rescued from the towns and districts captured, and little processions of these were straggling rearward out of range of the guns, and out of the way of the fighting troops. At times liberated Belgian women could see their sons, brothers or husbands going forward into battle. On October 17th the German retreat in Flanders became a rout. The enemy were fleeing rapidly on their entire front from the sea southward. The British entered Lille.

The Germans fled from Ostend and British naval forces were landed there. The Belgian infantry were sweeping up the coast, and Belgian patrols entered Bruges. In the afternoon of the day King Albert of Belgium, and Queen Elizabeth entered Ostend. The splendid fighting of the Belgian troops and their magnificent victory was now attracting universal attention. It was one of the revelations of the war. They were bearing the giant's share of the work of the Allied armies in their own

British Official Photograph

BELGIAN SOVEREIGNS RE-ENTER BRUGES

King Albert and Queen Elizabeth of Belgium saluting the Allied colors, on their triumphal entry into Bruges at the head of

BELGIUM'S EFFORT 137

country, and had already liberated territory which more than doubled the area of that part of Belgium which had been in their possession.

With the Belgian coast cleared of invaders it became open to British transports which would afford relief to the whole Allied armies from the resultant decrease in the congestion of the channel ports. On October 19th the progress continued. Zeebrugge was occupied by the Allies, the last Belgian port remaining in German hands.

The Belgian advance continued along the whole line. King Albert entered Bruges. Day after day the advance continued. The reception of the King and Queen of Belgium in the recovered towns was something to remember. In Bruges they rode in amid the tumultuous cheering of the frenzied population. In the central square they were received by the burgomaster with an escort of a solitary gendarme, who had refused to give up his uniform and old-fashioned rifle to the enemy; though fined and imprisoned he had kept their hiding place secret. As he stood there alone with fixed bayonet the King and the Queen shook him by the hand and congratulated him. Greatly moved, he stammered, "It is too great an honor, too great an honor."

And with all this happiness came the happiness arising from the return of the soldiers to the homes from which they had been absent so long, the reunions of husband and wife, of parents and children. Belgium was now to reap the reward for her heroism.

CHAPTER VIII

Italy's Terrific Drive

FOR many months after the great Italian stand on the Piave there was inactivity on both fronts in Italy. The Italians had been reenforced by troops from France and Great Britain and their own army was now larger than it had been at any other time. On June 15th, about the time when the Germans were being driven back on the Marne and the Oise, the Austrians, urged to action by the Germans, suddenly undertook a great offensive on a front from the Asiago Plateau to the sea, a distance of ninety-seven miles.

From the very start it was plain that the Italians were resisting magnificently. The offensive was not unexpected, either in time or locality, and had been openly discussed in the Italian press. The Italians therefore were not taken by surprise, and moreover since the disaster of Caparetto the Italians had learned by a patient campaign of education what they were fighting for.

On the second day of the battle the Austrian troops made a desperate effort to break through the Italian lines, particularly in the eastern sector of the Asiago Plateau, and crossed the Piave River at two places. They also attacked the French positions between Osteria di Monfenera and Maranzine, but were driven back with heavy loss. At every point where the Austrians were able to advance the Italians initiated vigorous counter attacks. The order to Italy's army was, "Hold at any cost."

On the third day of the battle the Austrian Offensive was being strongly checked. They had established three bridge heads on the Piave, but had not been able to advance. The most notable of these crossings was that in the Montello sector. Montello is of particular importance, because it is the hinge between the mountains and the Piave sectors of the Italian front. If it could be held the Austrians would

ITALY'S TERRIFIC DRIVE 141

be in a position to dominate from the flank and rear all the Italian positions defending the line of the Piave in the dead flat plain to the south.

On the Lower Piave the Austrians had made gains and had captured Capo Sile. The Austrians were using a million men and were using liquid fire and gas bombs, but their every move was resisted strongly. Vienna was claiming the capture of 30,000 men, but the Italian reports claimed that the Austrian losses were stupendous. Thousands of dead were heaped before the Italian line in the mountain sectors, blocking the mule paths and choking the defiles. No fewer than nine desperate onslaughts upon Monte Grappa, always with fresh reserves, were broken upon Grappa heights, with terrific losses.

On July 19th the dispatches from Rome were emphasizing the Italian counter attacks. Not only were the Italians preventing the enemy from making further gains, but they were beginning to crowd him back at the points where he had crossed the river, and were raining bombs and machine-gun bullets upon the

Austrian troops at the bridge head. They were also taking the initiative in the fighting in the mountain sectors.

By June 20th the Austrian defeat was clear. Their forces were backed against the flooded Piave, which had carried away their bridges and left them to the mercy of the Italians. Thousands were being killed and other thousands captured. Czecho-Slovak troops, it was reported, had joined in the fighting, and had given their first tribute of blood to the generous principles of freedom and independence for which they were in arms. In the Piave delta the Italians had regained Capo Sile, which had been captured early in the drive, and it was reported that all along the Piave line they had won complete control of the air, not a single Austrian machine being still aloft. The spirits of the Austrian troops had been definitely weakened. They were war wearied, and evidence began to accumulate that Austria's drive was a "hunger offensive."

As the battle continued reports began to arrive of the gallant deeds of American airmen,

ITALY'S TERRIFIC DRIVE 143

who were helping in the fighting along the front. The airmen were assisting in destroying the bridges that the Austrians were trying to throw across the river. The Piave was now a vast cataract and the bridges which it had not washed down were constantly destroyed by the aviators. The Austrians on the western bank were finding it difficult to obtain supplies and were resorting to hydroplanes for that purpose. On June 24th the Austrian attack had definitely failed and they were fleeing in disorder across the Piave. One hundred and eighty thousand men had already been lost and forty thousand were hemmed in on the western side of the river. The Austrian communications were emphasizing the difficulties they were meeting with through the heavy rains.

The victory of the Italians, which was now apparent, was received all over Italy with great public rejoicing. Italy had been repenting in sackcloth and ashes her defeat of the previous fall. Now they had made amends and were showing what the Italian soldier could really do. In America, and among the Allied

Powers, there was great enthusiasm, and Secretary of War Baker sent this congratulatory message to the Italian Minister of War:

> Your Excellency: The people of the United States are watching with enthusiasm and admiration the splendid exploits of the great army of Italy in resisting and driving back the enemy forces which recently undertook a major offensive on the Italian front. I take great pleasure in tendering my own hearty congratulations, and would be most happy to have a message of greeting and congratulation transmitted to General Diaz and his brave soldiers.
>
> NEWTON D. BAKER,
> Secretary of War of the United States.

In announcing to his victorious army the repulse of the Austrians General Diaz, the Italian Commander-in-Chief, said: "The enemy who, with furious impetuosity, used all means to penetrate our territory has been repulsed at all points. His losses are very heavy. His pride is broken. Glory to all commands, all soldiers, all sailors."

On the 26th of June the Italian troops, having forced the last rear guard of the retreating Austrians to surrender and completely occupied the west bank of the Piave, began an offensive on the mountain front in the Monte Grappe sector. They gained more than 3,000 prisoners, and considerable territory. On the southern part of the Piave front they were carrying on a vigorous offensive against the Austrian positions within the Piave delta. The Austrian troops, at that point, were being prevented from retreat by the high water, and suffered terrible losses. On July 6th the Italians drove the last of the enemy from the delta.

The campaign in Italy now languished, until on October 27th Italy began her last terrible drive. The great Italian Offensive was made not only by their own forces and the French and British troops, which had assisted them the previous June, but during the intervening period a large force of Americans had arrived in Italy. On June 27th Secretary Baker had made the announcement that General Pershing had been instructed to send into Italy a regiment that was then in training in France. The regiment thus sent was augmented considerably later. The purpose of sending troops to Italy, Mr. Baker explained, was rather political than military. It was desired to demonstrate again that the Allied nations and the United States were one in their purposes on all fronts, and to extend the intercourse between the troops of all the powers at war with Germany.

On the second day of the Italian offensive their success increased. More than nine thousand Austrians were taken prisoners and fifty-one guns were captured. The Piave River had been crossed, and the Italians had advanced four miles to its east. The attacks in the mountain region were being more bitterly contested, and counter attacks had enabled the enemy to regain some of their lost positions.

On October 30th the Italian advance was continuing. The Austrian front appeared to be breaking under the heavy blows of the Allied troops. Dispatches indicated striking successes, not only on the Italian front but at the points where the British and the French were holding the line. The Americans were being held in reserve, but American airplanes were

Photo by James H. Hare.

THE FIRST DAY ON THE PIAVE

ITALY'S TERRIFIC DRIVE 147

actively participating in the work at the front. By this time the last lines of the Austro-Hungarian resistance on the central positions along the Piave River had been broken, and more than fifteen thousand prisoners been taken. The Austrians, however, had been desperately resisting, and their artillery fire at many points was very effective, especially that which had been directed at the pontoon bridges thrown across the Piave.

King Victor Emanuel had been present in person during the crossing, and was often under the fire of the Austrian guns. On October 30th, 33,000 Austrians had been captured and the Italians had reached Vittorio. Americans had now joined in the fighting.

The Austrian retreat reached the proportion of a rout. They were still fighting, especially in the mountain region, but in the plains east of the Piave they were in full flight. Taking into consideration the numbers of troops in the Austrian lines and their apparently plentiful supplies, it began to seem probable that their break was due more to political maneuvers than to military force. The Austrians at this time were making a great peace drive, and the dissatisfaction at home had effected the morale of the troops at the front. The conditions in Italy were in close resemblance to those in Bulgaria just before Bulgaria applied for an armistice.

On the 1st of November the Austrians were completely routed, and were streaming in confusion down the valleys of the Alpine foothills, and fleeing northward for the Piave. Reports from Austria indicated riots at Vienna and Budapest. In Vienna people were parading the streets, shouting "Down with the Hapsburgs!" On October 29th, the Austrians asked for an armistice. Their announcement read as follows:

The High Command of the armies, early Tuesday, by means of a Parliamentaire, established communication with the Italian army command. Every effort is to be made for the avoidance of further useless sacrifice of blood, for the cessation of hostilities, and the conclusion of an armistice. Toward this step which is animated by the best intentions the Italian High Command at first assumed an attitude of unmistakable refusal, and it was only on the evening of Wednesday that, in accord with

Photo by James H. Hare.

AMERICAN TROOPS ON THE ITALIAN FRONT
Yanks marching in review on Columbus Day before Samuel Gompers, President of the American Federation of Labor.

ITALY'S TERRIFIC DRIVE 149

the Italian High Command, General Weber, accompanied by a deputation, was permitted to cross the fighting line for preliminary pourparlers.

General Diaz, the Italian Commander, had referred the Austrian request to the Versailles Conference, and had acted in accordance with their direction. In proposing the armistice the Austrians had also expressed their resolve to bring about peace and to evacuate the occupied territory of Italy. This was the beginning of the end.

The northern part of Italy is bounded by the Alps, and between those lofty ranges and the deep valleys there had been constant fighting. In this fighting, both on mountain and in valley, there were the most extraordinary deeds of individual heroism, constantly exhibited.

The Alpine regiments, known in Italy as the Alpini, were men of extraordinary physical powers, accustomed to mountain climbing, and filled with courage and patriotism. Owing to the nature of the territory in such contests, only a limited number of men could be used at one time, and the fighting went on over masses of snow or solid rock. Guns were hauled up precipices and dugouts excavated in the rock itself. The Italian troops, clothed in white overalls to prevent their being seen, moved with great rapidity from point to point, and forced their enemy to keep constantly on the alert. In the great Italian drive just described the most bitter fighting was that which occurred in these mountainous regions.

The work of the Italian aviators is also worthy of special attention. They not only secured entire command of the air, but by flying low they often threw into confusion with their machine guns the Austrian infantry. Their wonderful work in bringing in military information, and in bombing expeditions, was not excelled, if it was equaled, by the airmen of any other country. The Italian airplanes themselves were engineering triumphs. The inventive genius so notable in these days in Italy found expression in their development. Some of their machines were the biggest made during the whole war, and the long journeys

ITALY'S TERRIFIC DRIVE

made by such machines deserve special mention. The most interesting feat of this kind was performed on August 9th by the famous poet, Captain Gabrielle D'Annunzio. Accompanied by eight Italian machines, he flew to the city of Vienna, a total distance of 620 miles, and dropped copies of an Allied manifesto over the city. They crossed the Alps in a great wind storm at a height of ten thousand feet, and all but one returned safely. The manifesto, which was written by D'Annunzio reads as follows:

> People of Vienna, you are fated to know the Italians. We are flying over Vienna and could drop tons of bombs. On the contrary we leave a salutation and the flag with its colors of liberty. We Italians do not make war on children, the aged and women. We make war on your government, which is the enemy of the liberty of nations,—on your blind, wanton, cruel government, which gives you neither peace nor bread, and nurtures you on hatred and delusions. People of Vienna, you have the reputation of being intelligent, why then do you wear the Prussian uniform? Now you see the entire world is against you, do you wish to continue the war? Keep on, then, but it will be your suicide. What can you hope from the victory promised to you by the Prussian generals? Their decisive victory is like the bread of

the Ukraine,—one dies while awaiting it. People of Vienna, think of your dear ones, awake! Long live Italy, Liberty and the Entente!

It was said that copies of this proclamation in Vienna had a value of fifty dollars a copy. D'Annunzio's great fame had seized upon the popular imagination. His career in the war would have been interesting in itself, but when one recognizes that he was already a world figure, the greatest modern Italian dramatist and novelist, his life seems almost like a fairy story. Before the war began he made addresses all over his country, urging Italy's participation in the war, and when war was declared, to him, as much as to any other man, was due the credit. He entered the Navy, and has written some fascinating descriptions of his life on board ship. Later he joined the airplane corps, and now was showering down upon the gaping populace of Vienna appeals to rise against its Hapsburg masters. D'Annunzio was extraordinary in his literary career. He had been the poet of passion, a writer of novels and plays, which although artistic in the highest degree, showed him to be an egotist and a decadent. But long before the war he had tired of his erotic productions and had begun to write the praises of Nature and of heroes. He had been singing the praises of his country. "La Nave" symbolizes the glory of Venice. He had become more wholesome. War was making him not only a man but a hero.

Of course D'Annunzio was not the only great literary man who had left the study for the battle-field. Æschylus fought at Marathon and Salamis; Ariosto put down a rebellion for his prince between composition of cantos of Orlando Furioso; Sir Philip Sydney was scholar, poet and soldier, and many a soldier when his wars were over has turned to the labors of the pen. Yet it is not without surprise that one sees D'Annunzio join this distinguished company, and one's admiration grows as it becomes plain that he was not a mere poseur. He was a poet, but he was a soldier too. Not every great poet could drive an airplane to Vienna.

CHAPTER IX

BULGARIA DESERTS GERMANY

DURING the year 1916 there was little movement in the Balkans. The Allies had settled down at Saloniki and entrenched themselves so strongly that their positions were practically impregnable. These entrenchments were on slopes facing north, heavily wired and with seven miles of swamp before them, over which an attacking army would have to pass. It was obviously inadvisable to withdraw entirely the armies at Saloniki. So long as they were there it was possible at any time to make an attack on Bulgaria in case Russia or Roumania should need such assistance. And moreover, it was evident that it was only the presence of the Saloniki army that kept Greece neutral. During the year there were a few fights which were little more than skirmishes; almost all of the German soldiers had been withdrawn, and it was chiefly the Bulgarian army that was facing the Allies. On May 26th Bulgarian forces advanced into Greece and occupied Fort Rupel, with the acquiescence of the Greek Government.

The Greeks were in a difficult position. It was not unnatural that King Constantine and the Greek General Staff believed that the Allies had small chance of victory. Moreover, they had no special ambitions which could be satisfied by a war against the Central Powers. On the other hand, Turkey was an hereditary enemy, and the big sea coast would put them at the mercy of the British navy in case they should join their fortunes to those of Austro-Germany. To an impartial observer their policy of neutrality, if not heroic, was at least wise. The Greek Government, therefore, did its best to preserve neutrality. The surrender of Fort Rupel was not, however, a neutral act and roused in Greece a strong popular protest.

Venizelos, who at all times was strongly friendly to the Allies and who was the one great

Greek statesman who not only believed in their ultimate victory but who saw that the true interests of Greece were in Anatolia and the Islands of the Ægean, was strongly opposed to King Constantine's action. The Allies showed their resentment by a pacific blockade, to prevent the export of coal to Greece, with the object of preventing supplies from reaching the enemy. This led to a certain amount of excitement and the Allied embassies in Athens were insulted by mobs. The governments, therefore, presented an ultimatum commanding the demobilization of the Greek army, the appointment of a neutral Ministry, and the calling of a new election for the Greek Chamber of Deputies, as well as the proper punishment of those who were guilty of the disorder.

In substance, the Greeks yielded to the Allied demand, but before a new election could be held an attack by the Bulgarians on the 17th of August changed the situation. The Bulgarian armies entered deep in Greek territory in the eastern provinces and captured the city of Kavalla without resistance from the armies

BULGARIA DESERTS

of Greece. A portion of the Greek army at Kavalla surrendered and was taken to Germany as "guests" of the German Government.

This action of the Greek army led to a Greek revolution which broke out at Saloniki on the 30th of August. The King pursued a tortuous policy, professing neutrality and yet constantly bringing himself under suspicion. The Revolutionists organized an army and finally M. Venizelos, after strong efforts to induce the King to act, became the head of the Provisional Government of the Revolutionists. The Allies pursued a policy almost as tortuous as that of King Constantine. They could not agree among themselves as to the proper policy, and took no decided course. King Constantine apparently had the support of Russia and of Italy.

Meantime the fighting against Bulgaria was still proceeding. The main force of the Allies was directed against the city of Monastir, which, after considerable fighting, was captured on November 19th. This gave the Serbians possession of an important point in their own country and naturally proved a great stimulus to the Serbian armies.

From that time on, and during the year 1917, little was done. Minor offensives were undertaken, some of which, like the Allied attack upon Doiran, deserve mention, but on the whole the fighting was a stalemate. Meanwhile the action of the Greek Government had become so unsatisfactory that it was finally determined to demand the abdication of King Constantine, and on June 11th he found himself compelled to yield. In his proclamation he said:

> Obeying necessity of fulfilling my duty toward Greece, I am departing from my beloved country accompanied by the heir to the crown, and I leave my son Alexander on the throne. I beg you to accept my decision with calm.

Early the next morning the King and his family set sail for Italy on his way to Switzerland, where he became another "King in exile." His son Alexander accepted the throne and issued the following proclamation:

> At the moment when my august father, making a supreme sacrifice to our dear country, entrusted to me the heavy duties of the Hellenic throne, I express but

BULGARIA DESERTS

one single wish—that God, hearing his prayer, will protect Greece, that He will permit us to see her again united and powerful. In my grief at being separated in circumstances so critical from my well-beloved father I have a single consolation: to carry out his sacred mandate which I will endeavor to realize with all my power, following the lines of his brilliant reign, with the help of the people upon whose love the Greek dynasty is supported. I am convinced that in obeying the wishes of my father the people by their submission will do their part in enabling us together to rescue our dear country from the terrible situation in which it finds itself.

The whole country to all appearance received the abdication with satisfaction. On June 21st, M. Venizelos came to Athens and the Greek Chamber, which was illegally dissolved in 1915, was convoked and Venizelos once again became Prime Minister. At last he had succeeded, and he proceeded at once to join the whole of the Grecian forces to the cause of the Allies. Of all the statesmen prominent in the Great War, there was none more wise, more consistent or more loyal than the great Greek statesman.

For more than a year the Allied armies facing Bulgaria, remained upon the defensive when suddenly, on the 16th of September, 1918, in the midst of the wonderful movements that were forcing back the German armies in France, a dispatch was received from the Allied forces in Macedonia. The Serbian army, in co-operation with French and English forces, had attacked the Bulgarian positions on a ten-mile front, had stormed those positions and progressed more than five miles. On the next day news was received that the advance was continuing; that the Allies had occupied an important series of ridges, and had pierced the Bulgarian front; that more than three thousand prisoners had been captured and twenty-four guns. The movement took place about twelve miles east of Monastir and the ridge of Sokol, and the town of Gradeshnitsa were captured by the Allied troops.

It soon became evident that one of the most important movements in the whole war was being carried on. The Bulgarian armies were crumbling, and the German troops sent to aid them had been put to flight. The Allied troops had advanced on an average of ten miles and

BULGARIA DESERTS 161

were continuing to advance. The Serbs, fighting at last near their own homes, were showing their real military strength. Four thousand prisoners had been taken, with an enormous quantity of war supplies. The Bulgarian positions which had yielded so easily were positions which they had been fortifying for three years, and had been previously thought to be impregnable.

On September 23d it became evident that the retreat of the Bulgarians had turned into a rout. Notwithstanding reinforcements of Germans and Bulgars rushed down in a frantic effort to check them, the Allied armies were advancing on an eighty-five-mile front, crushing all resistance. The Italian army, on the west, was meeting with equal success, and the news dispatches reported that the first Bulgarian army in the region of Prilep had been cut off. A dispatch received by the British War Office reported "As the result of attacks and continual heavy pressure by British and Greek troops, in conjunction with the French and Serbian advance farther west, the enemy has evacuated his whole line from Doiran to the west of the Vardar." As it retreated the Bulgarian army was burning supplies and destroying ammunition dumps, burning railway stations and ravaging the country.

By this time it was felt throughout the Allied world that the Bulgarian defeat would have important political consequences. It was remembered that a short time before King Ferdinand had paid a visit to Germany, and after long conferences with the German War Lord, had hastily returned to Bulgaria. It was recalled that there had been many signs of serious disorder in Bulgaria, where the Socialist party had been in close touch with the advance parties in the Ukrainian Republic. It seemed possible that the Bulgarian defeats had been brought about by Bulgarian dissension and it was also evident that Germany was in no position to offer effective support to its Bulgarian accomplice.

As the days passed by the news from this front became more and more favorable. At all points the Bulgarian armies were retreat-

BULGARIA DESERTS 163

ing in the most disorderly manner, closely pursued by the Serbians, French, English, Italians, and Greeks. Bulgarian troops were deserting in thousands, and thousands of others were surrendering without resistance.

On September 26th it was announced that the Bulgar front had disappeared; that the armies had been cut into a number of groups and were fleeing before the Allied troops. Town after town was being captured, with enormous quantities of stores. On Friday, September 27th, it was announced that Bulgaria had asked the Allies for an armistice of forty-eight hours, with a view to making peace.

The situation was now causing intense excitement. The Germans tried to minimize the Bulgarian surrender. A dispatch from Berlin declared that Premier Malinoff's offer of an armistice was made without the support of other members of the Cabinet or of King Ferdinand, and that Germany would make a solemn protest against it. German newspapers were demanding that Malinoff be dismissed immediately and court-martialed for high treason. The Berlin message asserted that the Premier's offer had created great dissatisfaction in Bulgaria and that strong military measures had been taken to support the Bulgarian front. According to statements from Sofia it was added a counter-movement against the action of the Premier had already been set on foot. It was declared in Germany that the Premier's act was the result of Germany's refusal to send sufficient reinforcements to Bulgaria. Secretary Lansing made the announcement that the United States Government had received a proposal for an armistice.

It appeared that Bulgaria had been maneuvering toward peace for some time. The Bulgarians had foreseen their inability to meet the expected Allied attack, and had made every effort to obtain German reinforcements. Moreover, they were highly dissatisfied with the treatment they had received from Germany in connection with Bulgaria's dispute with Turkey as to territorial dispositions to be made after the war. Probably the most important reason, however, for the Bulgarian overthrow was that by this time they were sick of the war. They had not, in the first place, gone into it with any enthusiasm, and though they could fight bravely enough against their Serbian foe, no true Bulgarian could feel himself in a natural position facing his old-time Russian friend.

Bulgaria had come to the end. Malinoff, the Premier, had from the beginning been opposed to the war. Mobs in Sofia were demanding surrender. Ferdinand was compelled to give way to the wishes of his Cabinet and his people, and in spite of the fact that he had promised the Kaiser to remain faithful to the Alliance, he gave his consent to the movement for unconditional surrender.

An official Bulgarian statement read as follows: "In view of the conjunction of circumstances which have recently arisen, and after the position had been jointly discussed with all competent authorities, the Bulgarian Government, desiring to put an end to the bloodshed, has authorized the Commander-in-Chief of the army to propose to the Generalissimo of the armies of the Entente at Saloniki, a cessation of hostilities, and the entering into of negotiations for obtaining an armistice and peace. The members of the Bulgarian delegation left yesterday evening in order to get into touch with the Plenipotentiaries of the Entente belligerents." This statement was dated September 24th.

When the Bulgarian officers entrusted with the proposal for an armistice presented themselves at Saloniki, General d'Esperey gave the following reply: "My response cannot be, by reason of the military situation, other than the following. I can accord neither an armistice nor a suspension of hostilities tending to interrupt the operations in course. On the other hand, I will receive with all due courtesy the delegates duly qualified of the Royal Bulgarian Government." The Bulgarian delegates were General Lonkhoff, commander of the Bulgarian Second Army, M. Liapcheff, Finance Minister, and M. Radeff, a former member of the Bulgarian Cabinet.

On the evening of the 29th an armistice was

BULGARIA DESERTS 167

signed. The terms of the surrender were approved by the Entente Governments, and hostilities came to an end at noon on September 30th. The terms of the armistice were as follows:

> Bulgaria agrees to evacuate all the territory she now occupies in Greece and Serbia; to demobilize her army immediately and surrender all means of transport to the Allies. Bulgaria also will surrender her boats and control of navigation on the Danube, and concede to the Allies free passage through Bulgaria for the development of military operations. All Bulgarian arms and ammunition are to be stored under the control of the Allies, to whom is conceded the right to occupy all important strategic points. The military occupation of Bulgaria will be entrusted to British, French and Italian forces, and the evacuated portions of Greece and Serbia, respectively, to Greek and Serbian troops.

This armistice meant a complete military surrender, and Bulgaria ceased to be a belligerent. All questions of territorial rearrangement in the Balkans were purposely omitted from the Convention. The Allies made no stipulation concerning King Ferdinand, his position being considered an internal matter, one for the Bulgarians themselves to deal with.

The armistice was to remain in operation until the final general peace was concluded.

The request of Bulgaria for an armistice and peace, stunned Germany, which at that time was living in an atmosphere of political crisis and military misfortune. The German papers laid much of the blame on the desperate economic conditions in Bulgaria, which had been made worse by political strife.

After the Bulgarian collapse the Serbians, with the other Allied troops who had just captured Uskub, swept northward to drive the remaining Germans and Austrians out of Serbia and beyond the Danube. On October 13th they captured Nish, thus cutting the famous Orient railroad from Berlin to Constantinople. German authorities announced that henceforth trains on this line would run only to the Serbian border.

On October 4th King Ferdinand abdicated his throne in favor of his son Crown Prince Boris, and left Sofia the same night for Vienna. Before leaving he issued the following manifesto:

By reason of the succession of events which have occurred in my kingdom, and which demand a sacrifice from each citizen, even to the surrendering of oneself for the well being of all, I desire to give as the first example the sacrifice of myself. Despite the sacred ties, which for thirty-two years have bound me so firmly to this country, for whose prosperity and greatness I have given all my powers, I have decided to renounce the royal Bulgarian crown in favor of my eldest son, His Highness the Prince Royal Boris of Tirnovo. I call upon all faithful subjects and true patriots to unite as one man about the throne of King Boris, to lift the country from its difficult situation, and to elevate new Bulgaria to the height to which it is predestined.

Before signing his declaration of abdication he had consulted with the party leaders and received their approval. King Ferdinand had lost his popularity ever since it became apparent that he had made a mistake in siding with the Teutonic Powers. He was undoubtedly in fear that a revolution might upset the whole dynasty. Premier Malinoff announced the abdication to the Bulgarian Parliament, and the accession of Prince Boris to the throne was received with much enthusiasm. The church bells were rung, and great crowds gathered in the streets.

Speaking from the steps of the Palace the new King said: "I thank you for your manifestation of patriotic sentiments. I have faith in the good star of Bulgaria, and I believe that the Bulgar people, by their good qualities and co-operation, are directed to a brilliant future." King Ferdinand, it was given out, had renounced politics and was intending in the future to devote himself to his favorite pursuits, chiefly to botany.

The surrender of Bulgaria was at once recognized as the overthrow of Germany's "Mittel-Europa" threat, which had apparently been carried into effect when Turkey and Bulgaria joined the Central Powers. It had for a long time been one of Germany's most coveted aims. After the Franco-Prussian war the German people had grown enormously in wealth and in numbers. It had become one of the greatest manufacturing powers in the world. Its ships were transporting its commerce on every sea, but it was not satisfied. The German leaders, most of whom were young men at the time of the war with France, and had been deeply im-

BULGARIA DESERTS

pressed by a sense of the German power, were full of the idea that Germany was the greatest of nations, and that she should impress her will on all the world.

They might have done this peacefully, for the seas were free, but German self-esteem was not satisfied with peaceful progress. They felt that it was necessary to reach out in the world for colonies. They seized a province in China. They meddled with affairs in Morocco. They annexed colonies in Africa, but none of these projects were wholly satisfactory. They provided no great outlet for the products of their workshops, nor for their overflow population, which largely went to North and South America and became citizens of these foreign nations.

Their eyes finally turned to the great East. There in China and India and the neighboring countries were three hundred millions of men whose trade would be a worthy prize for even Germany's ambition. Then began the development of what is sometimes called Germany's Mittel-Europa dream. Her scholars encouraged it; her travelers brought reports which stimulated the interest, and soon she began practically to carry it into effect. It meant the building of a great railroad down to the Per-

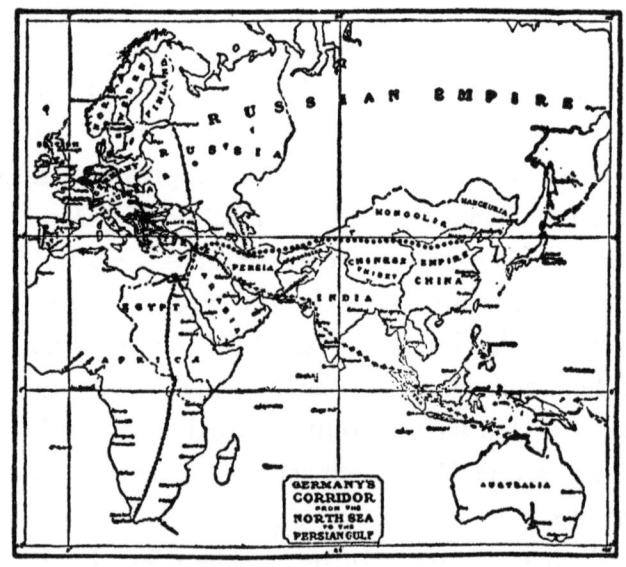

HOW THE PAN-GERMANS PLANNED TO EXTEND THEIR "MITTEL-EUROPA" DREAM

sian Gulf; a railroad to be controlled by nations where her influence would be all-powerful. She needed Austria, she needed Serbia, she needed Bulgaria and Turkey.

At first the project was carried out peacefully. Friendly relations were stimulated with Turkey and the other necessary powers; permits were obtained to build the railroad. But Germany was not the only power that had dreamed this dream. Alexander the Great had done it. Napoleon had done it, and England had carried it out. From the days of Queen Elizabeth the English control of India was one of its greatest assets.

Through most of the nineteenth century the English power in the East was threatened, not by Germany, but by Russia. It was because of this threat that England had always protected Turkey. Turkey and Constantinople were her barrier against Russia. The literature of England in the last days of the nineteenth century shows clearly her fear of Russian intrigues in India. Kipling's Indian stories are full of it. But now that fear had passed. It was no longer the imaginary danger which might come from the great Slavic Empire, but a trade weapon in the grasp of the most efficient military power ever developed that was threatening. Against this threat

England had been doing her best. Here and there near the Persian Gulf she had been extending her influence. Here and there, as German Consuls obtained concessions, they would find them later withdrawn, because England had stepped in. Yet just before the war, England, anxious for peace, had come to an agreement with Germany practically admitting the German plans to be carried out as far as Bagdad.

It looked as though it were only a question of time, but when the Balkan wars established Serbia as the greatest of the Balkan powers, and gave Russia a preponderating influence among the Balkan nations, and when it began to look as if some great Balkan state might be established which should be friendly to Russia and consequently a hindrance to the German scheme, then it was that it was necessary that war should come. The Germans had been wonderfully successful. For a time they controlled Austria, Bulgaria, Serbia and Turkey, but with Bulgaria's fall the end of the Mittel-Europa dream had come.

CHAPTER X

THE CENTRAL EMPIRES WHINE FOR PEACE

THE Allied victories in France during the months of August and September of 1918, led to a new peace offensive among the Central Powers. It was very plain to the German High Command, as well as to the Allied leaders, that Germany's great ambitions had now been definitely thwarted. It seems clear that, in spite of the hopeful and encouraging words which they addressed to their own armies, the expert soldiers, who were controlling the destinies of Germany, understood well the conditions they were facing. Putting aside all sentiment, therefore, they deliberately set out to obtain a peace which would leave them an opportunity to gain by diplomacy what they were sure that they were about to lose on the field of battle. They had made pleas for peace before, but their pleas had been rejected.

The Allied leaders were fighting for a principle. They could not be satisfied with a draw. They could not be satisfied if Germany were left in a position which would enable her after a rest of a few years to renew her effort to impose her will upon the world. It was unanimously recognized that the war must be carried on to the very end. The Allies took this position when the fortunes of war seemed to have gone against them, when Russia was defeated, Roumania and Serbia crushed, and the German lines in France were approaching the capital. It was unlikely that now, when Germany was suffering defeat and every day was yielding the Allied armies encouraging gains, there should be any change in the strong determination of the Allied leaders. Nevertheless, it was necessary to make the attempt.

On September 15th, the Austro-Hungarian Government addressed a communication to the Allied Powers and to the Holy See suggesting a meeting for a confidential and non-binding discussion of war aims, with a view to the possible calling of a peace conference.

THE WHINE FOR PEACE 177

The official communication from the Austro-Hungarian Government was handed to Secretary of State Lansing in Washington at 6.20 o'clock on September 16th.

At 6.45 the following abbreviated reply of the United States Government was made public, by the Secretary of State:

> I am authorized by the President to state that the following will be the reply of this government to the Austro-Hungarian note proposing an unofficial conference of belligerents. "The Government of the United States feels that there is only one reply which it can make to the suggestion of the Austro-Hungarian Government. It has repeatedly and with entire candor stated the terms upon which the United States would consider peace, and can and will entertain no proposal for a conference upon the matter concerning which it has made its position and purpose so plain."

Arthur J. Balfour, the British Foreign Secretary, in a statement made September 16th said: "It is incredible that anything can come of this proposal. . . . This cynical proposal of the Austrian Government is not a genuine attempt to obtain peace. It is an attempt to divide the Allies." Premier Clemenceau in France took similar grounds, and stated in the

French Senate: "We will fight until the hour when the enemy comes to understand that bargaining between crime and right is no longer possible. We want a just and a strong peace, protecting the future against the abominations of the past." Italy joined with her Allies and declared that a negotiated peace was impossible.

The refusal on the part of the Allies to respond to the Austrian peace proposal evidently greatly disturbed the German leaders. The continued German reverses, and the surrender of Bulgaria had taken away all hope. They were anxious to conclude some kind of peace before meeting irretrievable disaster. They therefore determined to appoint as Chancellor of the Empire some statesman who might be represented as a supporter of an honest peace, and Count von Hertling, whose previous utterances might put under suspicion any peace move coming from him, was removed and Prince Maximilian of Baden appointed as his successor on September 30th.

Prince Maximilian was put forward as a

THE WHINE FOR PEACE

Moderate, in accordance with the evident purpose of the government to continue peace proposals. He was the heir apparent to the Grand Ducal throne of Baden, and was the first man in public life in Germany to declare that the Empire could not conquer by the sword alone. He did this in an address to the Upper Chamber in Baden, of which he was President, on December 15, 1917. "Power alone can never secure our position," he said, "and our sword alone will never be able to tear down the opposition to us."

At the same time he made an attack upon the ideals set up by President Wilson. "President Wilson," he continued, "after three years of war gathers together all the outworn slogans of the Entente of 1914, and denounces Germany as the disturber of the peace, proclaiming a crusade for humanity, liberty and the rights of small nations." Then, forgetting that the United States had entered the war nearly a month after the abdication of the Czar of Russia, he added: "President Wilson has no right to speak in the name of democracy and liberty, for he was the mighty war ally of Russian Czardom, but he had deaf ears when the Russian democracy appealed to him to allow it to discuss peace conditions." The Baden address created a great sensation all over Germany, which was increased when in an interview in January he declared that all ideas of conquest must be abandoned, and that Germany must serve as a bulwark to prevent the spread of Bolshevism among the western nations.

There can be no doubt that the appointment of Prince Maximilian was a definite attempt to seek peace. It was thought that he would be recognized by the Allied leaders as an honest friend of peace, and that any effort he would make would be treated with respect. He was, however, a vigorous supporter of the Kaiser and of German autocracy, and while his appointment might mean that Germany was desirous of peace it did not mean that she had changed her ways. Three days before the appointment of Prince Maximilian, President

THE WHINE FOR PEACE

Wilson in an address delivered in the Metropolitan Opera House in New York, had restated the issues of the war, declaring (1) for impartial justice, (2) no leagues within the common family of the league of nations, (3) no selfish economic combination within that league, and (4) all international agreements and treaties of every kind must be made known in their entirety to the rest of the world.

Prince Maximilian, coming into power undoubtedly for the purpose of arranging a peace, proceeded at once to make a new peace offer. He based his action on President Wilson's speech and on October 4th sent to President Wilson, through the Swiss Government, the following note:

> The German Government requests the President of the United States to take in hand the restoration of peace, acquaint all the belligerent states with this request, and invite them to send plenipotentiaries for the purpose of opening negotiations. It accepts the program set forth by the President of the United States in his message to Congress on January 8th, and in his later pronouncements, especially his speech of September 27th, as a basis for peace negotiations. With a view to

avoiding further bloodshed the German Government requests the immediate conclusion of an armistice on land and on water and in the air.

He followed this note on October 5th with an address before the German Reichstag, of which the following are the most important points:

In accordance with the Imperial decree of September 30th, the German Empire has undergone a basic alteration of its politic leadership. As successor to Count George F. von Hertling, whose services in behalf of the Fatherland deserve the highest acknowledgment, I have been summoned by the Emperor to lead the new government. In accordance with the governmental method now introduced I submit to the Reichstag, publicly and without delay, the principles by which I propose to conduct the grave responsibilities of the office. These principles were firmly established by the agreement of the federated governments and the leaders of the Majority Parties in this honorable House before I decided to assume the duties of Chancellor. They contain therefore not only my own confession of political faith, but that of an overwhelming portion of the German people's representatives—that is, of the German nation—which has constituted the Reichstag on the basis of a general, equal, and secret franchise and according to their will.

Only the fact that I know the conviction and will of the majority of the people are back of me, has given me strength to take upon myself conduct of the Empire's affairs in this hard and earnest time in which we are

THE WHINE FOR PEACE 183

living. One man's shoulders would be too weak to carry alone the tremendous responsibility which falls upon the government at present. Only if the people take active part in the broader sense of the word in deciding their destinies, in other words, if responsibility also extends to the majority of their freely elected political leaders, can the leading statesman confidently assume his part of the responsibility in the service of folk and Fatherland.

My resolve to this has been especially lightened for me by the fact that prominent leaders of the laboring class have found a way in the new government to the highest offices of the Empire. I see therein a sure guarantee that the new government will be supported by the confidence of the broad masses of the people, without whose true support the whole undertaking would be compelled to failure in advance. Hence what I say today is not only in my own name, and those of my official helpers, but in the name of the German people.

The program of the majority parties, upon which I take my stand, contains first, an acceptance of the answer of the former Imperial Government to Pope Benedict's note of August 1, 1916, and an unconditional acceptance of the Reichstag resolution of July 19th, the same year. It further declares willingness to join the general league of nations based on the foundation of equal rights for all, both strong and weak. It considers the solution of the Belgian question to lie in the complete rehabilitation of Belgium, particularly of its independence and territorial integrity. An effort shall also be made to reach an understanding on the question of indemnity.

The program will not permit the peace treaties hitherto concluded to be a hindrance to the conclusion of the general peace. Its particular aim is that popular representative bodies shall be formed immediately on a broad basis in the Baltic provinces, in Lithuania and Poland. We will promote the realization of necessary preliminary conditions therefore without delay by the introduction of civilian rule. All these lands shall regulate their constitutions and their relations with neighboring peoples without external interference.

He went on to point out the progressive political developments in Prussia and declared that the "Message of the King of Prussia promising the democratic franchise must be fulfilled quickly and completely."

President Wilson did not find Prince Maximilian's proposal wholly satisfactory, and on October 8th he sent a reply in which, after acknowledging the receipt of the proposal, he inquired of the Imperial Chancellor whether the meaning of the proposal was that the German Government accepted the terms laid down in his address to the Congress of the United States and in subsequent addresses; and whether its object in entering into discussions would be only to agree upon the practical de-

THE WHINE FOR PEACE 185

tails of their application. He also suggested that so long as the armies of the Central Powers were upon the soil of the governments with which the United States was associated, he would not feel at liberty to propose a cessation of arms to those governments. He also inquired whether the Imperial Chancellor was speaking merely for the constituted authorities of the Empire, who had so far conducted the war.

President Wilson's reply aroused much difference of opinion among the Allies, but on the whole was regarded as a clever diplomatic move.

The German Government responded to these questions of the President on October 12th, by a message signed by Dr. W. S. Solf, who had just been appointed Imperial Foreign Secretary. In this reply the German Government declared that it did accept President Wilson's terms; that it was ready to comply with the suggestion of the President and withdraw its troops from Allied territory, and that the

German Government was representing in all its actions the will of the great majority of the German people.

Germany had, indeed, made enormous concessions, and the German people appeared to have taken for granted that such an offer would be accepted. An Amsterdam despatch declared: "People in Berlin are kissing one another in the street, though they are perfect strangers and shouting peace congratulations to each other. The only words heard anywhere in Germany are 'Peace at last.'"

The President, however, had been struck by the news coming in from day to day of new atrocities in France, and of new cases of submarine murders, and in his reply of October 14th, he declared that while he was ready to refer the question of an armistice to the judgment and advice of military advisers of the government of the United States and the Allied governments, he felt sure that none of those governments would consent to consider an armistice as long as the armed forces of Germany continued the illegal and inhuman practices which they were persisting in. He also emphasized the fact that no armistice would be accepted that would not provide absolutely satisfactory safeguards and guarantees of the maintenance of the military supremacy of the armies of the United States and of the Allies in the field. The President also called the attention of the Government of Germany to that clause of his address on the Fourth of July in which he had demanded "the destruction of every arbitrary power that can separately, secretly and of its single choice disturb the peace of the world, or, if it cannot be presently destroyed, at least its reduction to virtual impotency." He declared that the power which had hitherto controlled the German nation was of the sort thus described, and that its alteration actually constituted a condition precedent to peace.

This answer of the President was greeted with approval in the United States and everywhere in the Allied countries. It meant that the Imperial Power of Germany was not to be allowed to hide itself behind a so-called reorganization done under its own direction. As one of the Senators of the United States expressed it: "It is an unequivocal demand that the Hohenzollerns shall get out."

During these negotiations the Allied armies under Marshal Foch had been driving the enemy before them. When Baron Burian was making his peace offer on behalf of Austria-Hungary the Americans were engaged in pinching off the St. Mihiel salient, and about that date the British were launching their great attack on the St. Quentin defenses. The reports of the great Allied drive indicated a constant succession of Allied victories.

On September 19th, the British advanced into the Hindenburg line, northwest of St. Quentin, and on September 20th, while the American guns were shelling Metz, the British were advancing steadily near Cambrai and La Bassée.

Day by day the advance proceeded. On September 26th, the first American army smashed through the Hindenburg line for an average gain of seven miles, between the Meuse and the Aisne Rivers on a twenty-mile front. On September 27th, the French gained five miles in an advance east of Rheims, and the British were attacking in the Cambrai sector on a fourteen-mile front, crossing the Canal du Nord and piercing the Hindenburg line at several points. On September 28th, the Americans reached the Kriemhilde line, while the British were close in on Cambrai. On September 30th, the British took Messines Ridge, while the French were still advancing between the Aisne and Vesle Rivers. On October 1st, the French troops entered St. Quentin and the British took the northern and western suburbs of Cambrai. During the next week an enveloping movement was instituted north and south of Lille. On October 5th, the Germans evacuated Lille, on October 9th the British took Cambrai.

In these drives the American colored troops played a conspicuous part. The entire Three hundred and sixty-fifth regiment, composed wholly of colored troops, was later awarded the coveted Croix de Guerre, or War Cross, by the French Government. It was a well-deserved honor, for the boys of the Three hundred and sixty-fifth bore themselves with great gallantry in the September and October offensive in the Champagne sector and suffered heavy losses. In conferring the Croix de Guerre, the citation dealt in considerable detail with the valor of particular officers and praised the courage and tenacity of the whole regiment.

The Germans were retreating in Belgium day by day, under the attacks of the Belgian and French armies. On October 11th the Germans evacuated the Chemin des Dames. On October 16th the Germans began the evacuation of the Belgian coast region and each day increased the number of Belgian towns once more in Allied control.

CHAPTER XI

BATTLES IN THE AIR

HE who conquers the fear of death is master of his fate. Upon this philosophy fifty thousand young men of the warring nations went forth to do battle among the clouds. The story of these battles is the real romance of the World War. In 1914 no one had ever known and history had never recorded a struggle to the death in the air. When the war ended a new literature of adventure had been created, a literature emblazoned with superb heroisms, with God-like daring, and with such utter disdain of death that they were raised out of the olden ranks of mere earth-crawling mankind and became supermen of the air.

Some of these heroic names became household words during the war. These were the aces of the French, American and German airforces. The British adopted a policy in news concerning their airmen similar to that governing their publication of submarine sinkings. They argued that the naming of British, Canadian and Australian aces would direct the attacks of German aviators against the most useful men in the British forces. They also felt that publicity would tend toward the swagger which in English slang was "swank" and toward a deterioration in discipline.

Raoul Lufberry, Quentin Roosevelt, son of ex-President Roosevelt, and Edward Rickenbacher were names that figured extensively in news of the American Air forces.

Lufberry and Roosevelt were killed in action. Rickenbacher, after dozens of hair-raising escapes from death, came through the war without injury. The pioneer of American aviators in the war was William Thaw of Yale, who formed the original Lafayette Escadrille.

Besides these men, America produced a number of other brilliant aces, an ace being one who brought down five enemy planes, each victory being attested by at least three witnesses.

BATTLES IN THE AIR 193

The French had as their outstanding aces Georges Guynemer and Rene Fonck. Guynemer went into the flying game as a mechanician. He became the most formidable human fighting machine on the western front before he was sent to death in a blazing airplane.

Lieut. Rene Fonck ended the war with a total of seventy-five official aerial victories. He had an additional forty Huns to his credit but not officially confirmed. His greatest day was when he brought down six planes. His quickest work was the shooting down of three Germans in twenty seconds.

He fought three distinct battles in the air when, on May 8, 1918, he brought down six German airplanes in one day. All three engagements were fought within two hours. In all, Fonck fired only fifty-six shots, an average of little more than nine bullets for each enemy brought down—an extraordinary record, in view of the fact that aviators often fired hundreds of rounds without crippling their opponent.

The first fight, in which Lieutenant Fonck

brought down three German machines, lasted only a minute and a half, and the young Frenchman gained his victory at the expense of only twenty-two shots.

Fonck was leading two other companions on a patrol in the Moreuil-Montdidier sector on May 8th, when the French squadron met three German two-seater airplanes coming toward them in arrow formation. Signaling to his companions, Lieutenant Fonck dived at the leading German plane and with a few shots sent it down in flames. Fonck turned to the left, and the second enemy flier followed in an effort to attack him from behind, but the Frenchman made a quick turn above him and, with five shots, sent the second German to death. Ten seconds had barely elapsed between the two victories.

The third enemy pilot headed for home, but when Lieutenant Fonck apparently gave up the chase and turned back toward the French lines the German went after him, and was flying parallel and a little below, when Fonck made a quick turn, drove straight at him and

© *Illustrated London News.*

PICKING ONE "OFF THE TAIL"

The German Albatross airplane going down in flames was in pursuit of the light British "Quirk" machine seen on the left, when suddenly a British Nieuport (at the right) dived through the clouds. The Albatross nose-dived, the British following with his guns working, and soon the German burst into flames and crashed to earth, his pursuer straightening out on his course.

sent him down within half a mile of the spot where his two comrades hit the earth.

The German heroes were the celebrated Captain Boelke, and the no less famous inventor of the "flying circus," Count von Richthofen. Captain Boelke caused a great many Allied "crashes" by hiding in clouds and diving straight at planes flying beneath him. As he came within range, he opened up with a stream of machine-gun bullets. If he failed to get his prey, his rush carried him past his opponent into safety. He rarely re-attacked. Count von Richthofen was responsible for many airplane squadron tactics that later were used on both sides. The planes under his command were gaily painted for easy identification during the thick of a fight. Their usual method was to cut off single planes or small groups of Allied planes, and to circle around them in the method employed by Admiral Dewey for the reduction of the Spanish forts and ships in the Battle of Manila Bay.

The dangers of aerial warfare were instrumental in producing high chivalry in all the encampments of airmen. Graves of fallen aviators were marked and decorated by their former foes and captured aviators received exceptionally good treatment, where foemen aviators could procure such treatment for them.

Until the advent of America into the war, neither side had a marked advantage in aircraft. At first Germany had a slight advantage; then the balance swung to the Allied side; but at no time was the scale tipped very much. American quantity production of airplanes, however, gave to the Entente Allies an overwhelming advantage. Final standardization of tools and design for the "Soul of the American Airplane" was not accomplished until February, 1918. Yet within eight months more than 15,000 Liberty engines, each of them fully tested and of the highest quality, were delivered.

The United States did not follow European types of engines, but in a wonderfully short time developed an engine standardized in the most recent efficiency of American industries.

According to Secretary of War Baker, an

inspiring feature of this work was the aid rendered by consulting engineers and motor manufacturers, who gave up their trade secrets under the emergency of war needs. Realizing that the new design would be a government design and no firm or individual would reap selfish benefit because of its making, the motor manufacturers, nevertheless, patriotically revealed their trade secrets and made available trade processes of great commercial value. These industries also contributed the services of approximately two hundred of their best draftsmen. Parts of the first engine were turned out at twelve different factories, located all the way from Connecticut to California. When the parts were assembled the adjustment was perfect and the performance of the engine was wonderfully gratifying.

Thirty days after the assembling of the first engine preliminary tests justified the government in formally accepting the engine as the best aircraft engine produced in any country. The final tests confirmed the faith in the new motor.

British and French machines as a rule were not adapted to American manufacturing methods. They were highly specialized machines, requiring much hand work from mechanics, who were, in fact, artisans.

The standardized United States aviation engine, produced under government supervision, said Secretary of War Baker, was expected "to solve the problem of building first-class, powerful and yet comparatively delicate aviation engines by American machine methods—the same standardized methods which revolutionized the automobile industry in this country."

The manufacture of De Haviland airplanes equipped with Liberty motors was a factor in the war. One of these De Havilands without tuning up, made a non-stop trip on November 11, 1918, from Dayton, Ohio, to Washington, D. C., a distance of 430 miles, in three hours and fifty minutes. Great battle squadrons of these De Haviland planes equipped with Liberty motors made bombing raids over the German lines in the Verdun sector. Others oper-

BATTLES IN THE AIR 199

ated as scouting and reconnaissance planes and as spotters for American artillery.

In the period from September 12th to 11 o'clock on the morning of November 11th, the American aviators brought down 473 German machines. Of this number, 353 were confirmed officially. Day bombing groups, from the time they began operations, dropped a total of 116,818 kilograms of bombs within the German lines.

Bombing operations were begun in August by the 96th Squadron, which in five flying days dropped 18,080 kilograms of bombs. The first day bombardment group began work in September, the group including the 96th, the 20th and 11th Squadrons. The 166th Squadron joined the group in November.

In twelve flying days in September the bombers dropped 3,466 kilograms of bombs; in fifteen flying days in October 46,133 kilograms, and in four flying days in November, 17,979 kilograms.

On November 11th, the day of the signing of the armistice, there were actually engaged on the front 740 American planes, 744 pilots, 457 observers and 23 aerial gunners.

Of the total number of planes, 329 were of the pursuit type, 296 were for observation and 115 were bombers. In addition, several hundred planes of various types were being used at the instruction camps when the war ended.

America, although the last of the great nations to embark upon a great aircraft production program, was the birthplace of the airplane, the Wright brothers being the undisputed inventors of the modern type.

Wilbur and Orville Wright made their first experiments in flying at Kittyhawk, N. C. Their first attempts were of a gliding nature and were accomplished by starting from the top of a dune or sandhill, the operator lying full length, face downward on the under plane of the machine. During these experiments they succeeded in flying six hundred feet.

Their first flight with an airplane driven by a motor was on December 17, 1903, when they succeeded in flying about two hundred and seventy yards in fifty-nine seconds. This ma-

BATTLES IN THE AIR

chine was driven by a sixteen-horse-power motor.

Santos Dumont was one of the early pioneers in aeronautical experiments. After showing a marked talent with balloons, he turned his attention to heavier-than-air machines, and in 1906 created a world's record in a flight of 230 yards at a speed of twenty-five miles an hour.

In 1907 Henry Farnum made a half circular flight in a Voisin biplane, using a fifty-horse-power motor, returning to his starting point. About this time a flight of nine minutes and fifteen seconds was recorded by Delagrande on a Voisin constructed biplane.

The first previously announced public flight was made on July 4, 1908, by Glenn H. Curtiss at Hammondsport, N. Y., and was witnessed by a number of New Yorkers who had gone to Hammondsport to see the flight.

In the winter of 1913–14 Mr. Rodman Wanamaker gave Glenn H. Curtiss a commission to build a flying boat which would fly across the Atlantic. Commander Porte was brought from England, and he, with Mr. Curtiss, worked out the designs for a flying boat much larger than any previously built, and fitted with two motors instead of one. As entirely separate power plants would be used, one motor would naturally run somewhat faster than the other, and it was freely predicted that the machine could not be handled. The first trial, however, proved that it would not only fly, but that after it was once in the air, one motor could be slowed down and even stopped and the machine continue to fly. This machine was the forerunner of the seaplane, used by the American, British and other navies in the war, although somewhat changed in detail. The beginning of the war stopped the transatlantic experiments and this machine found its way into the British navy. It was christened the "America," and the larger flying boats or seaplanes which are now being built and used by the British and American navies are still known as the "America" or super-American type.

At first fighting operations were carried out by individual aviators or comparatively small squadrons, but the battles of March, 1918, wit-

BATTLES IN THE AIR

nessed the definite development of larger squadrons, maneuvering as effectively as bodies of cavalry, and in massed formation attacking infantry columns. The possibilities of the new aerial arm were further demonstrated in the creation of a barrage, as effective as that of heavy artillery, for the purpose of holding back advising bodies of infantry.

In the first days of the German offensive there took place an aerial battle which up to that time was unique in the annals of warfare.

It was a battle not merely for the purpose of gaining the mastery of the air, but to aid Allied infantry and artillery in stemming the tide of the German advance, and when the drive finally slowed down and came to a halt in Picardy, the Allied airmen had undoubtedly contributed largely to the result.

During March 21 and 22, 1918—the opening days of the great German drive—there was comparatively little aerial activity. The aviators of both sides were preparing for the impending battle, which actually began on the morning of March 23d and lasted all that day and the day following.

The story of the air battle of March 23d-24th reads like one of the most extraordinary adventure tales ever imagined. The struggle began with squadrons of airplanes ascending and maneuvering as perfectly as cavalry. They rose to dizzy heights, and, descending swept the air close to the ground. The individual pilots of the opposing sides then began executing all manner of movements, climbing, diving, turning in every direction, and seeking to get into the best position to pour machine-gun fire into enemy airplanes. Every few minutes a machine belonging to an Allied or German squadron crashed to the ground, often in flames. At the end of the first day's fighting wrecked airplanes and the mangled bodies of aviators lay strewn all over the battle-field.

All next day, March 24th, the struggle in the air went on with unabated fury. The Allied air squadrons were now on the offensive and penetrated far inside the German lines. The German aviators counter-attacked whenever

BATTLES IN THE AIR

they could, and more than once succeeded in crossing the French lines. But at the close of the second day victory rested with the Allied airmen, and during the next five scarcely a German airplane took the air.

The sudden termination of the war caused speculation throughout the world concerning the future of the airplane. When rumor declared that America's newly-won pre-eminence in aviation would disappear, Captain Roy N. Francis, of the Division of Military Aeronautics, made this statement:

> America cannot afford to junk the airplane fleet which has cost her so many millions of dollars. I do not believe that any other nation will do so. Even if the peace congress should decide on universal disarmament, there are still any number of uses to which airplanes can be put in time of peace.
>
> Take the air mail service, for instance. This is now only in its infancy, but it is destined to become as common as the railway mail service. It will employ hundreds of airplanes and aviators all over the country.
>
> Then there is the possibility of our machines being used for sea-coast patrol work, a valuable addition to our coast-guard forces which save many ocean vessels from disaster every year.
>
> They will be largely used for army dispatch work.

Instead of sending official messages from post to post by the present methods, airplanes will be used after the war as they are now being used at the front.

On the Great Lakes, airplanes can be used for coast-guard work, as on the seacoast, and they can also be used for patrolling the lakes themselves. Think how many wrecked lake vessels might have been saved in the past had there been an airplane nearby to carry its message of distress and guide rescue ships to the scene.

Forest patrol is still another opening for the use of expert aviators. Every year, almost, our great forest fires in the northwest demonstrate that our present methods of prevention of forest fires are faulty; chiefly because the fires are not discovered while they are still smoldering. Constant airplane patrol over our great forests would make forest fires a thing of the past.

Then there are any number of commercial uses to which airplanes can be put. Instead of a cargo of bombs, a commercial airplane could carry a cargo of small package freight for which immediate delivery is necessary.

The use of the airplane for passenger carrying is now being developed. The huge Caproni and Handley-Page machines will be used for this purpose in the future. Thousands of persons will want to fly just for the novelty, and the possibility of accidents will be reduced to the minimum.

Again, there is the need for scientific research and improvement of the airplane, which will keep scores of men and machines busy for years.

It will not be necessary, of course, to maintain the numerous government training fields for aviators after

BATTLES IN THE AIR   207

the war, but some of the best of them should be retained. I do not believe it will be necessary to discharge a single pilot or observer from the army or to junk a single undamaged airplane after the war.

Henry Woodhouse, Governor of the Aero Club of America and a world-wide authority on aeronautics, made the following forecast:

Aircraft capable of lifting fifteen tons, with a speed of one hundred miles an hour, are now in actual production. The first of the American-built Caproni planes, equipped with four Liberty motors and developing 1,750 horse-power has just been successfully tested. This giant plane has a total lifting capacity of 40,000 pounds, or twenty tons. The super-Handley-Page or the Caproni could easily carry fifty bags, or more than a ton of mail. This means 100,000 letters. Judging the future development of aircraft by what has taken place in the last two years, we may look for the building of a 5,000-horse-power airplane, possibly within a year.

If the people of the various cities along the eight great air-ways already proposed insist on it, at least a dozen additional aerial mail lines can be established within twelve months. This can be done by utilizing only machines not needed by the army or navy. That means it will be possible to send by postplane at least 50,000,000 of the 100,000,000 day and night letters, and at least 25,000,000 of the 50,000,000 special delivery letters that are sent each year in the United States.

Postoffice officials estimate that the average cost of telegraphic day and night letters now going over the wires is close to one dollar each. Special delivery letters average about thirteen cents apiece.

This makes a total of more than fifty million dollars' worth of potential aerial mail business that is simply waiting for the establishment of aerial mail routes which can easily be established within the next twelve months.

Four hundred miles is the distance over which postplane day mail is most effective. Aerial mail letters are effective over any distance, since, with proper stations, light signals and guides for night postplane flying, the air mail can be carried more than one thousand miles between the hours of 6 P. M. and 8 A. M.

The cost of aerial mail night and day letters will be less than that of wire communication. The cost of an aerial mail letter is sixteen cents for two ounces. For this price there can be sent a message that would cost five dollars to send by telegraph.

The estimate of $50,000,000 of potential postplane business takes no account of the possibilities of transporting parcel post aerial mail. One of the Caproni 2,100-horse-power machines now in operation could easily transport 2,500 pounds of mail. At least $25,000,000 worth of parcel post could be sent by airplane.

Enthusiasts who look forward to the transatlantic transportation of aerial mail as certain to come within the next twelve-month assert that there is another twenty-five million dollars' worth of transatlantic mail waiting for an aerial mail service. They point out that Uncle Sam now pays eighty cents a pound to American steamships to carry transatlantic mail and that a charge of $1 per letter across the Atlantic would be a paying proposition.

BATTLES IN THE AIR 209

Charges of mismanagement and graft were investigated by the United States Senate and by the Department of Justice. Former Justice of the United States Supreme Court Charles E. Hughes was named by President Wilson to conduct the latter inquiry. Waste was found, due largely to the emergency nature of the contract. Justice Hughes recommended that Col. Edward Deeds, of the United States Signal Corps, be tried by court martial for his connection with certain contracts, and recommended that several other persons be tried in the United States courts. Justice Hughes and the Senate Investigation Committee gave their unqualified approval to the management of America's aircraft production by John D. Ryan. Mr. Ryan resigned his charge as head of the Aircraft Production Board in November, 1918. His last public announcement was of the invention of an aerial telephone, by which the commander of a squadron standing on the ground could communicate with aviators flying in battle formation.

CHAPTER XII

HEALTH AND HAPPINESS OF THE AMERICAN FORCES

SINCE the fateful day when Cain slew Abel, thereby setting a precedent for human warfare, no fighter has been so well protected from disease and discomfort of mind and body, so speedily cured of his wounds, as the American soldier and sailor during the World War.

The basis of this remarkable achievement was sanitary education preached first by competent physicians and sociologists; then by newspapers to the civilian population; and ultimately by the soldiers and sailors themselves, each man acting as an evangel of personal and community health and sanitation. In 1914, before war was declared, the words "venereal diseases" were relegated to the advertisements of quacks and patent medicines. When the

HEALTH OF THE FORCES 211

war ended, virtually every young and old man and woman knew the meaning of the words and the miseries that come in their train. So it was with other details of the care of the human body, with sewage problems, with the grave community question of pure water, with the use of intoxicating beverages, and with other problems inter-woven with the health and happiness of humanity.

Among the leaders in this wide-flung campaign of education was the American Red Cross. Starting with a mere nominal membership before the war, its roster rose to the mighty total of more than 28,000,000 American men, women and children when the war ended. More than $300,000,000 was poured into the American Red Cross treasury. In addition to these contributions of money, came the free services of millions of Americans, mostly women. Red Cross workshops dotted the land, and from these came bandages, sweaters, comfort-kits, trench necessities, clothing for homeless refugees, and a vast quantity of material aid in every conceivable form.

American Red Cross workers during the war knitted 14,089,000 garments for the army and navy. In addition, the workers turned out 253,196,000 surgical dressings, 22,255,000 hospital garments and 1,464,000 refugee garments. Sewing chapters repaired old clothing and sent it overseas to the orphaned and the widowed, and millions of Americans learned the sublime lesson of sacrifice through the Red Cross—a lesson that left its imprint upon America for generations.

The work of the American Red Cross extended through many lands. It followed the flags of the Entente Allies into Palestine, Mesopotamia, India, South Africa, and other battle-grounds. Its work on the western front was a miracle of achievement. In Russia through the Red Terror of the Revolution the workers of the American Red Cross went serenely about their tasks of mercy, relieving the hungry, aiding the sick, and clothing the ragged peasants.

Henry P. Davidson left the firm of J. P. Morgan & Company to devote his administra-

HEALTH OF THE FORCES 213

tive genius to the affairs of the American Red Cross. Other men and women of rare executive ability joined in the free tender of their services to the work of the Red Cross.

While the organization strove mightily against famines, wounds and disease overseas, it was suddenly confronted during the period from September 8th to November 9th, 1918, with the severest epidemic America had experienced in generations. Returning American troops brought the germs of the malady known as "Spanish influenza" into New York and Boston. Thence it spread throughout the country. During its brief career the epidemic claimed a total of 82,306 deaths in forty-six American cities, having a combined population of 23,000,000. Philadelphia, a great center of war industry, with the Philadelphia Navy Yard harboring thousands of sailors and marines, showed the highest mortality in proportion to population, 7.4 per 1,000; Baltimore with 6.7 per 1,000 showed the next greatest mortality.

The record of the Red Cross in this epidemic

was one of instant service. Hundreds of thousands of masks were made in Red Cross workrooms, and these were worn by nurses and by members of families in afflicted homes.

On May 1, 1917, just before the appointment of the War Council, the American Red Cross had 486,194 members working through 562 chapters. On July 31, 1918, the organization numbered 20,648,103 annual members, besides 8,000,000 members of the Junior Red Cross—a total enrolment of over one-fourth the population of the United States. These members carried on their Red Cross work through 3,854 chapters, which again divided themselves into some 30,000 branches and auxiliaries.

The total actual collections from the first war fund amounted to more than $115,000,000. The subscriptions to the second war fund amounted to upward of $176,000,000. From membership dues the collections approximated $24,500,000.

The Home Service of the Red Cross with its more than 40,000 workers, extended its ministrations of sympathy and counsel each month to upward of 100,000 families left behind by soldiers at the front.

Supplementing, but not duplicating, the work of the American Red Cross, were the services of the Y. M. C. A., Y. W. C. A., Knights of Columbus, Jewish Welfare Association, Salvation Army, American Library Association and other bodies.

These operated under the general supervision of the War and Navy departments: Commissions on Training Camp Activities. Raymond B. Fosdick was the chairman of both these bodies. Concerning these commissions, President Wilson declared:

> I do not believe it an exaggeration to say that no army ever before assembled has had more conscientious and painstaking thought given to the protection and stimulation of its mental, moral and physical manhood. Every endeavor has been made to surround the men, both here and abroad, with the kind of environment which a democracy owes to those who fight in its behalf. In this work the Commissions on Training Camp Activities have represented the government and the government's solicitude that the moral and spiritual resources of the nation should be mobilized behind the troops. The

country is to be congratulated upon the fine spirit with which organizations and groups of many kinds, some of them of national standing, have harnessed themselves together under the leadership of the government's agency in a common ministry to the men of the army and navy.

Afloat and ashore the organizations operating under the supervision of the two commissions gave to the men of the American forces home care, suitable recreation, and constant protection. The club life of the army and navy, both in the training camps and after the men went into the service, was most capably directed by the Y. M. C. A., Knights of Columbus, and the Jewish Welfare Association. Non-sectarianism was the rule in all of the huts and clubs conducted by these organizations. Catholic, Protestant and Jewish chaplains mingled with workers of the Salvation Army, with professional prize-fighters who became athletic instructors, with actors and actresses who contributed their talents freely to the entertainment of soldiers and sailors. Moving-picture shows, boxing contests, continuation schools, canteens where women workers served American-made dishes—these were some of the

© *Press Illustrating Service.*

THE Y. M. C. A. IN THE FRONT LINE TRENCHES

The Y. M. C. A. sign beside the trench points the way to a dugout, instead of the usual hut, in which soldiers found the comforts which made the sign of the triangle famous.

HEALTH OF THE FORCES 217

activities following the men. The Y. M. C. A. and Knights of Columbus bore the largest share of this work. More than $300,000,000 was contributed by the people of America to the maintenance of these activities.

The other organizations rounded out the work of the first two organizations and filled in with special attention to needs on which the others did not specialize.

The larger organization, the Y. M. C. A., was chosen by the government to carry out a portion of the government program—the conducting of the canteens.

The Knights of Columbus specialized in comforts less considered by other war relief organizations.

Nothing gave greater relaxation to the fighting man, coming from the trenches, or the battle line caked with mud and blood and weary with long hours, than a shower bath, and generous facilities were provided close to the fighting front.

Back of the lines in the rest billets and concentration camps, provisions were less generous than at the front until the Knights of Columbus took up the task of seeing that the men who were temporarily away from the active fighting had these facilities for bathing. It was but one of the many activities of the Knights of Columbus, but one of the most appreciated.

One of the first requisitions made by Rev. John B. De Valles, one of the first chaplains sent over by the Knights of Columbus, was for a shower bath and he set it up in connection with his headquarters in a little French town and it was overworked from the first. From this spread the movement for establishing shower baths in club houses being opened behind the lines and in villages.

There was no preaching in a Knights of Columbus hall or club room, but there was clean moral environment and healthy recreation and amusement, for this was proven the thing to keep up the morale of fighting men.

The Y. M. C. A. built 1,500 huts in Europe costing from $2,000 to $20,000 each, equipped with canteen, reading and writing and recre-

HEALTH OF THE FORCES 219

ational facilities to soldiers. It operated twenty-eight different leave areas with hotels that had a total of 35,000 beds. In addition, in Paris, port towns, and several big centers in the war zone there were "Y" hotels for transient soldiers where one could get a clean bed and a good meal at about half the price charged by French hotels. Over 3,000 movie and theatrical shows a week were provided free, and 300 "Y" athletic directors had charge of the sports in the American army, operating 836 athletic fields. Enormous quantities of cookies and chocolate and cigarettes were supplied.

A hundred of the best known educators from America directed educational work. The staff consisted of Professor Erskine of Columbia University, Professor Daly of Harvard, Professor Coleman of Chicago University, Professor Appleton of the University of Kansas and Frank Spaulding, superintendent of the Cleveland public schools.

Seconding the work of the Y. M. C. A., its sister organization, the Y. W. C. A., extended its activities from the training camps of America to the battle-fields of Europe.

At the close of its first year of America's participation in the war, the Y. W. C. A. had six established lines of work in France: Hostess Houses, clubs for French working women and business girls, clubs for nurses with the American army, clubs for women of the signal corps, clubs for British women (Waac's) working with the American army, and recreation work for all women employed in any way by the American Expeditionary Force. In one year its activities spread to twenty-five cities, and it had forty-three units.

The Hostess Houses were at Paris and Tours. The Hotel Petrograd, on the Rue Caumartin, was leased in Paris and turned out to be one of the most interesting centers of American life in France. It was run on the most liberal lines, in a thoroughly democratic way. The meals were good and in the big dining-room men were admitted on the same footing as women. There were two of these Hostess Houses at Tours.

HEALTH OF THE FORCES 221

For the girls of the signal corps twenty-two homes were opened and there were huts for the Waacs at Bourges and Tours. Y. W. C. A. secretaries were attached to twenty base hospital units and opened fourteen clubs for nurses.

The most interesting and unique work of the Y. W. C. A. was that of its foyers for French working women and business girls. There were thirteen of these in Lyons, Rouen, Bourges, Tours, Ste. Etienne, Paris and Mont Lucon.

The Salvation Army erected hotels at the various large training camps in America, and its workers made American doughnuts for the soldiers close to the battle-lines in France. The work done by the men and women of the Salvation Army aided materially in bringing the heart of America into France.

The Jewish Welfare Association not only performed notable service in following the men from training camps into actual service, but it also planned and executed a great reconstruction program under the direction of Felix M.

Warburg, chairman of the Joint Distribution Committee.

The American Library Association solved the grave problem of providing the soldiers and sailors with suitable reading matter. Each of the cantonments had its special library building in charge of a trained librarian, and interesting literature followed the men into the field through the services of this organization.

Some idea of the work of these various organizations is gained by reading the following order received by Raymond B. Fosdick at his headquarters in Washington after the steamship Kansas carrying supplies for the various huts at American field quarters, was sunk:

> Send 20 tons plain soap, 20 tons condensed milk, 10 tons chocolate, 5 tons cocoa, 2 tons tea, 5 tons coffee, 5 tons vanilla wafers, 50 tons sugar, 20 tons flour, 2 tons fruit essences, 2 tons lemonade powder, 120,000 Testaments, 120,000 hymn-books, tons of magazines and other literature, 30 tons writing-paper and envelopes, 50,000 folding chairs, 500 camp cots, 2,000 blankets, 20 typewriters, 60 tents, 75 moving-picture machines, 200 phonographs, 5,000 records, 1 ton ink blotters, $75,000 worth athletic goods, 30 automobiles and trucks.

The order was filled at once.

Besides the associations above enumerated, other volunteer organizations contributed to the health and happiness of American soldiers and sailors. The Emergency Aid of Pennsylvania established two clubs, one in Paris, the other in Tours, both of which performed notable services in feeding and restoring the spirits of American soldiers and sailors. The club in Paris was under the direction of the Rev. Frederick W. Beekman and that at Tours was directed by Amos Tuck French. Mrs. Barclay Warburton of Philadelphia was designated by Governor Brumbaugh as Commissioner-General of Overseas Work for the Emergency Aid. Other states had similar organizations looking after the comfort of the men.

But it was upon the professional doctors, nurses and sanitarians that the bulk of the task devolved. This task included the prevention as well as the cure of maladies menacing the American forces. It reached out into years after the war into the problems of re-education and re-habilitation of the shell-shocked and the wounded. Major-General William C. Gorgas, former Surgeon General of the Army, stated this concept when he said:

"The whole conception of governmental and national responsibility for caring for the wounded has undergone radical change during the months of study given the subject by experts serving with the Medical Officers' Reserve Corps and others consulting with them. Instead of the old idea that responsibility ended with the return of the soldier to private life with his wounds healed and such pension as he might be given, it is now considered that it is the duty of the government to equip and re-educate the wounded man, after healing his wounds, and to return him to civil life ready to be as useful to himself and his country as possible."

To carry out this idea reconstruction hospitals were established in large centers of population. Boston, New York, Philadelphia, Baltimore, Washington, Buffalo, Cincinnati, Chicago, St. Paul, Seattle, San Francisco, Los Angeles, Denver, Kansas City, St. Louis,

Memphis, Richmond, Atlanta and New Orleans were sites of these institutions. Each was planned as a 500-bed hospital but with provision for enlargement to 1,000 beds if needed.

These hospitals were not the last step in the return of the wounded soldiers to civil life. When the soldiers were able to take up industrial training, further provision was ready.

Arrangements were made by the Department of Military Orthopedics to care for soldiers, so far as orthopedics (the prevention of deformity) was concerned, continuously until they were returned to civil life. Orthopedic surgeons were attached to the medical force near the firing line and to the different hospitals back to the base orthopedic hospital which was established within one hundred miles of the firing line. In this hospital, in addition to orthopedic surgical care, there was equipment for surgical reconstruction work and "curative workshops" in which men acquired ability to use injured members while doing work interesting and useful in itself. This method supplanted the old and tiresome one of prescribing a set of motions for a man to go through with no other purpose than to re-acquire use of his injured part.

Instructors and examiners for all the troops were furnished by the Department of Military Orthopedic Surgery. A number of older and more experienced surgeons acted as instructors and supervisors for each of the groups into which the army was divided.

A peculiar condition arising from the use of heavy artillery in the war was that called "shell-shock."

The most pathetic wrecks of war were soldiers suffering from shattered nerves. Paris had many of them. They appeared to be normal. But they were human wrecks.

Shell-shock or the aftermath of illness from wounds left them in weakened health, subject to violent heart attacks. Most of them lacked energy and perseverance. They became awkward, like big children. If employment was found for them—for many had large families to support—they quickly lost their jobs through apathy or collapse.

A society in Paris did everything possible to relieve the sufferings of these victims of the war. It operated with the authorization of the French Government under the name "L'Assistance aux Blessés Nerveux de la Guerre."

American hospitals after the war contained many of these cases. Some of the victims became incurably insane.

Besides the noble work done by the great army of American physicians, surgeons and nurses, in caring for soldiers and sailors, a service of scarcely less magnitude was rendered to the civilian populations of France, Belgium and Italy. Tuberculosis in France was a real plague, taking a toll of 80,000 lives every year. American physicians and nurses preached the doctrine of fresh air, care of the teeth and proper food for children. Almost immediately this campaign of sanitation had its effect in a decreasing death-rate from tuberculosis.

European nations generally were benefited by the stay of the American army overseas.

The straightforward manner in which the social evil was attacked had direct benefits. The important detail of dental care also received an interest through the advent of the American soldier. The London *Daily Mail* made this comment on that question:

"One thing about the American soldiers and sailors must strike English people when they see these gallant fighters, and that is the soundness and general whiteness of their teeth. From childhood the 'Yank' is taught to take care of his teeth. He has 'tooth drill' thrice daily and visits his dentist at fixed periods, say, every three or four months. If by chance a tooth does decay, the rot is at once arrested by gold or platinum filling. American dentists never extract a tooth. No matter how badly decayed it may be, they save the molar by crowning it with gold.

"The United States soldiers have set us a splendid example in this matter. They fairly shame the ordinary 'Tommy' by the brilliance of their molars."

Lightning Source UK Ltd.
Milton Keynes UK
UKHW01f0808200618
324522UK00001B/33/P